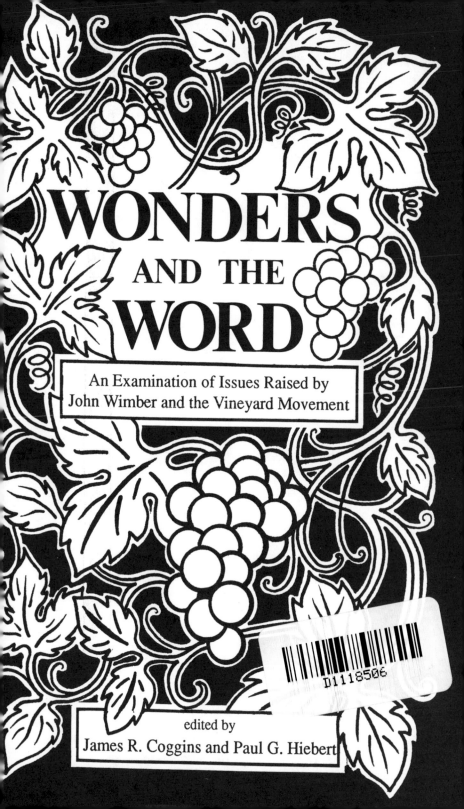

WONDERS
AND THE
WORD

An Examination of Issues Raised by
John Wimber and the Vineyard Movement

edited by
James R. Coggins and Paul G. Hiebert

WONDERS
AND THE
WORD

edited by

James R. Coggins

Paul G. Hiebert

Kindred Press

Winnipeg, MB   Hillsboro, KS

Published simultaneously by Kindred Press, Winnipeg Manitoba, R2L 2E5 and Kindred Press, Hillsboro, Kansas 67063.

Cover Design by Fred Koop, Winnipeg, MB

Canadian Cataloguing in Publication Data

Main entry under title:

Wonders and the word: an examination of issues raised by John Wimber and the Vineyard movement

Bibliography: p.
ISBN: 0-919797-82-2

1. Pentecostalism. 2. Wimber, John. I. Coggins, James Robert, 1949-. II. Hiebert, Paul G., 1932-.
BR1644.W653 1989   270.8'2   C89-098072-1

Printed in Canada by The Christian Press, Winnipeg

International Standard Book Number: 0-919797-82-2

TABLE of CONTENTS

List of Contributors

James R. Coggins, an editor with the *Mennonite Brethren Herald* for the past five years, has a Ph.D. in history from the University of Waterloo, Waterloo, ON.

Paul G. Hiebert is professor of mission anthropology in South Asian Studies at Fuller Theological Seminary, Pasadena, CA.

Abraham Friesen is professor of history at the University of California in Santa Barbara, CA.

Victor G. Doerksen is professor and head of the Department of German at the University of Manitoba, Winnipeg, MB.

Levi Keidel is head of the Missions Department at Columbia Bible College, Clearbrook, BC.

Don Lewis is assistant professor of church history at Regent College in Vancouver, BC.

John Vooys teaches New Testament and theology at Columbia Bible College, Clearbrook, BC.

John Schmidt is academic dean at Columbia Bible College, Clearbrook, BC.

Tim Geddert is assistant professor of New Testament at Mennonite Brethren Biblical Seminary, Fresno, CA.

J.B. Toews is professor emeritus of history and theology at Mennonite Brethren Biblical Seminary, Fresno, CA.

Art Glasser is professor of mission theology at Fuller Theological Seminary, Fresno, CA.

FOREWORD

"Christians should not throw stones at each other." Many supporters of the Vineyard movement have questioned our decision to write a book critiquing John Wimber and his ideas. Indeed, we have heard such sentiments so often that we have begun to recognize them as a sort of Vineyard slogan, almost as identifiable as "signs and wonders." Still, it is a good question. Why write a book critiquing a movement that has brought revival to many church members, brought salvation to many unbelievers, performed miracles and glorified God? Why not leave the movement to carry on its good work in peace? There are several reasons.

A Cold and Lifeless Orthodoxy?

The first reason for not leaving John Wimber and the Vineyard movement alone is that they will not leave us alone. Wimber directs his appeal to Christians, advertises in other churches and asks for the cooperation of other churches in supporting his seminars. When the Vineyard movement moved into southern British Columbia, for instance, it did so with the qualified support of some other denominations. One pastor with some charismatic leanings reported that he had promoted a "signs and wonders" seminar in his congregation. It was advertised as a nondenominational ministry designed to bring revival to the churches, much like a Billy Graham crusade—and he had encouraged some of his members to attend. After a second seminar, the movement started setting up Vineyard churches in the area and attracting those who had been blessed by the seminars. The pastor felt betrayed. Rather than bring revival to his congregation as had been promised, the seminars brought division. The interdenominational seminars had seemed a ploy to start a new denomination.

The history of the church in dealing with new movements and ideas is not a happy one. Blistering tracts, often written by second-rank theologians, denounced new ideas as heresies and assailed the characters of their adherents. Frequently, violent actions followed the violent words. In the Roman Empire after Constantine, dissidents from the established church were removed from office and banished from their homes. In the Middle Ages and after, the level of violence increased. John Hus was burned at the stake; Martin Luther was condemned to death; the Anabaptists were slaughtered by the thousands.

In contrast, perhaps because we have learned something from history, there has been a reluctance on the part of many church people to criticize the Vineyard movement lest we find ourselves to be "fighting against God" (Acts 5:39). One after the other, the writers of the articles in this volume have urged us to make sure that we are fair and balanced in our approach. Meanwhile, John Wimber, while arguing that it would be unbrotherly and unloving of us to criticize him, has often characterized other churches with uncomplimentary phrases like "inactive audience," "cold and lifeless orthodoxy," "wicked in its pride and separation," and "unbelieving and perverse."

We have been conditioned by the existence of a multitude of denominations, burdened by a modern attitude that allows people to do their own thing and fearful of being guilty of the oppression practised by established churches in the past. Afraid that we might be accused of oppressing and suppressing dissidents by force, we have abdicated our responsibility to lovingly discipline erring members of our churches. Afraid of appearing judgmental, we have not dared to offer loving, brotherly advice to other Christian movements such as the Vineyard movement. Afraid of appearing arrogant, we have failed to stand for the truth as we see it, or even to express our opinions.

Scripture makes it clear, however, that we are to test all teaching to discern what is of God. But it is difficult to undertake rigorous biblical thinking in times of enthusiasm, when those involved see all questioning as lack of faith and evidence of "cold and lifeless orthodoxy." Jonathan Edwards, who himself was involved in a great revival, cautioned:

> They looked upon critical enquiries into the difference between true grace and its counterfeits . . . to be impertinent and unseasonable; tending rather to damp the work of the Spirit of God than promote it; diverting their own minds and the minds

of others, as they supposed, from that to which God at such an extraordinary time did loudly call them . . . . The cry was, "Oh, there is no danger, if we are but lively in religion and full of God's Spirit and lively faith . . . . If we do but follow God there is no danger of being led wrong! Let us press forward and not . . . hinder the good work by . . . spending time in these criticisms and carnal reasonings!" This was the language of many, until they ran on deep into the wilderness, and were caught by the briars and thorns of the wilderness.[1]

Theological debate is not sin. It is a part of the process whereby the church works out the implications of the salvation brought by Jesus Christ. It is this task we are engaged in throughout this book.

Dividing the Sheep

Throughout the history of the church, Jesus' prayer "that all of them may be one" (John 17:21) has haunted serious church people. Contrary to the assumptions of some historians, the church was never really united in an organizational sense. It had grown too quickly and spread too far for that. Still, there was a sense that the church, at least in a given geographical area ("the church of God in Corinth," for example), should be united. The church in history has never achieved unity, any more than it has achieved a perfect understanding of doctrine or a perfectly holy manner of living in a sinful world. Nevertheless, church unity has remained an ideal of the church, just as holiness and understanding remain ideals. Church people have striven to unite where they can and to cooperate where they cannot unite.

Many leaders of dissident reform movements in the past have had a deep concern for the unity of the church. In starting the Reformation, Martin Luther appealed to the pope and the bishops to implement the reforms he had found in scripture. It was only after he had been repudiated, condemned, expelled and forbidden to speak that he established the Lutheran church—and he always remained uncomfortable with that development. The Anabaptists in Zurich at first appealed to the authorities of church and state to carry the Reformation farther. Two years later they were expelled from Zurich and forbidden to teach. It was only then that they began to practise believer's baptism, a reform they had urged for the whole church. In response, they were hunted down, imprisoned, tortured and martyred by the thousands. In the eighteenth century, John Wesley sought to have his converts and new congregations incorporated into the Church of England. He refused for decades to organize the Methodist church formally as a separate denomination. It was only after repeated rebuffs that he finally gave in and recognized his exclusion from the Anglican church.

In contrast, some members of the Vineyard movement have shown an almost callous disregard for the unity of the church. New adherents have swelled the Vineyard fellowships, experiencing joy, fulfillment and love, but leaving in their wake a trail of shattered dreams, hurt feelings and broken relationships. There have been few, if any, talks with churches and denominations from whom the Vineyard fellowship has actively recruited members and whole churches. Such results cannot be wiped away by offhand comments to the effect that church splits are good for growth.

Divisions in the church are sometimes necessary when a dead orthodoxy continues to resist the life of the Spirit. However, splits should be approached with great reluctance and with great sorrow at the apostasy that has befallen Christ's church. Moreover, there should be the desire to continue discussions with that church. Our second reason for writing this book is dismay at unnecessary brokenness in the church.

Picking up the Pieces

While the first two reasons for writing this book come from a concern for the church, the third flows from a pastoral concern for individuals within the church.

John Wimber is a man endowed by God with some special gifts. He is a revivalist, a healer and an inspiring worship leader. He is not a deep thinker or infallible teacher. This is why we can affirm his ministry (or at least many aspects of it) and yet remain troubled by some aspects of his teaching. There is a dangerous tendency in our age to seek infallible gurus, faultless leaders, and follow them blindly. Professional athletes who have been Christians for two years become our role models. Evangelists are asked to advise us on theology. Professional Christian singers become our Bible teachers. Perhaps John Wimber is not the best person to explain the work the Holy Spirit is doing through him. For this, it may be better to turn to those who have been given the gifts of teaching and discernment, such as the collection of Christian scholars who have consented to contribute to this book.

Elsewhere in this book, Tim Geddert writes, "Simple answers are so attractive, but when they fail in the crisis, then who will pick up the pieces?" It is the "pieces" this book is written for, not the people who have been blessed by the Vineyard movement, but those who have found its answers and theology inadequate, those whom God did not choose to bless with signs and wonders, those who are disillusioned, confused and despairing. To the theology of the miraculous must be added the theology of divine providence and discipleship. We believe in a God of miracles. But we also believe in a sovereign God who sometimes (and sometimes inexplicably) says no. We write this book for those who have heard the answer no, to help rescue them from the despair of excessive expectations in a fallen world and to point out that God is still a God of yes.

Fighting against God

Finally, we write this book for those who have shunned John Wimber as a false prophet and condemned his movement as demonic. God is working through John Wimber, and we want to affirm this. There are things we can learn from him. There are many places, too many places, where the church is marked by "a cold and lifeless orthodoxy" and is in need of revival. We write lest church members overreact to the Vineyard's excesses and refuse to have anything to do with spiritual gifts and so lack the ministry God intends them to have.

Expounding the Truth

This book was born out of confrontation, the challenge John Wimber and his Vineyard movement have posed to mainline,

Anabaptist and evangelical churches in general (and to the Mennonite Brethren church in particular, to which several of the writers of this volume belong). But hopefully, in the end this book is not about John Wimber. The apostle Paul wrote no tracts attacking heresies. He wrote pastoral epistles expounding the truth. It is the intent of the writers of this book not to concern themselves primarily with the minor question of whether John Wimber (or any of us) is right or wrong. Rather, this book concentrates on the ideas raised by Wimber. It deals with the important questions of how we relate to the Lord Jahweh, Creator of heaven and earth, his beloved Son and our Savior, Jesus Christ, and the inestimable blessing of his Holy Spirit.

Part One

INTRODUCTORY CONSIDERATIONS

Who is John Wimber? What has he done? What has he said? What has he written? What is the Vineyard movement? We provide here a brief introduction.

To further illustrate the Vineyard phenomenon, we also include a varied collection of first-person accounts of individuals' experiences with the Vineyard movement.

The Man, the Message and the Movement

James R. Coggins and Paul G. Hiebert

What is the Signs and Wonders movement? What is a Vineyard fellowship? Where did the movement come from and where is it going? The answers to these questions are tied up with the life story of the movement's founder and leader, John Wimber.

John Wimber was a successful rock musician, composer and record producer. At age 29 he was converted to Christ. For a while he worked in a factory and then in a psychiatric ward. He studied sociology and theology, graduating from a Bible college associated with the Evangelical Friends (a conservative Quaker group). He became pastor of a Quaker church in Yorba Linda, California. The church was growing, but Wimber became disillusioned. In 1975 he left the pastorate and began working with the Fuller Evangelistic Association as a lecturer on church growth.

A Fuller Experience

Wimber's association with Fuller Theological Seminary in Pasadena, California was pivotal in his future direction. Fuller Seminary was founded by Charles E. Fuller in the 1940s to train evangelists and to bridge the gap between fundamentalists and mainline denominations.[1] Later a well-respected psychology school was added to the theology school. Finally, in 1965, the School of World Mission was founded under the directorship of Donald McGavran. McGavran originated the church growth school of thought. He began studying successful churches and formulated principles on what made them grow. The School of World Mission became a well-known department, training church leaders from North America and around the world. A parallel resource was the Fuller Evangelistic Association, a separate organization also founded by Charles E. Fuller, originally to continue his evangelistic radio broadcasts. Later the FEA discontinued the radio broadcasts and shifted its focus to providing consultation services to local churches. John Wimber served on one of several FEA teams of experts that traveled widely, consulting, analyzing local churches and offering advice on how to foster growth. Such teams perhaps served as a model for later Vineyard teams, which travel widely offering seminars and teaching on Vineyard emphases.

As important as this practical training was, equally important were the theological influences that Wimber imbibed through Fuller professors.

From George Eldon Ladd, Wimber gained his understanding and emphasis on the kingdom of God. For Ladd, the kingdom of the world was under the dominion of Satan, afflicted with natural catastrophes, bondage to sin, sickness, demons and death. Jesus, however, came proclaiming the kingdom of God, rebuking storms, healing the sick, casting out demons and raising the dead. Jesus' followers are to follow in his footsteps, performing the same works and proclaiming the presence of the kingdom.

Another source that Wimber has quoted extensively was an article by Paul Hiebert, a professor in Fuller's School of World Mission. In the article, Hiebert pointed out the need for missionaries to deal with questions of ancestors, spirits, healing, food, guidance and other existential problems for which people seek answers in folk religions.[2] Wimber also encountered students at Fuller from third world countries who reported experiences of healings and other miracles. Wimber began to wonder if the experiences were transferable to North America. He came to believe that miracles did not happen in scientific, materialistic North America because they were not expected here. From this he began to draw the conclusion that miracles are readily available to all believers but only a lack of faith prevents them from occurring.

Wimber also latched onto the idea of a "power encounter" between the forces of darkness and the gospel (just as Elijah had confronted the prophets of Baal in I Kings 18). This idea had been popularized by Dr. Allen Tippet, who had worked for many years as a missionary in the Solomon Islands and had also taught at Fuller.[3] Such power encounters are common in countries where Christian missionaries confront animistic religions.

Perhaps the biggest influence on Wimber, however, was Peter Wagner, who replaced McGavran in the church growth chair at the School of World Mission in 1981.

A Charismatic Direction

When they met, neither Wimber nor Wagner was a charismatic. Wagner had actively opposed Pentecostalism while a missionary in Bolivia.[4] Wimber had evidently spoken in tongues and prayed for his son's healing shortly after his conversion, but had been dissuaded by his wife from practising such gifts.[5] However, both Wagner and Wimber began to move in a charismatic direction. Wagner was influenced by Tippet and others at Fuller. Perhaps more decisive for him, however, was the inherent pragmatism in the church growth ideology. Pentecostal churches were undoubtedly growing very quickly, and Wagner tended to approve of anything that promoted church growth. Wagner later came to characterize Wimber's movement as the "third wave" of a broad spiritual revival in the twentieth century. The first had been Pentecostalism in the early years of the century, and the second had been the charismatic movement in the 1960s.[6] The growth of all three waves has been phenomenal. In 1958 there were about 12,000,000 Pentecostals in the world. By 1977 there were over 50,000,000 Pentecostals and charismatics. By 1987, with the third wave giving added impetus, the total was estimated at 277,000,000, including 20,000,000 in non-charismatic churches. In fact, Pentecostal-charismatic Christians now represent 17.5 percent of the world's 1,646,000,000 Christians.[7]

Wimber's movement in a charismatic direction began with

disillusionment with his work with the Fuller team. As fruitful as these years were, Wimber began to have doubts. On his travels, he encountered churches that were looking for gimmicks and mechanical processes to make the church grow, rather than revival and the power of the Holy Spirit.[8] (This is a criticism that has been leveled at the church growth movement on a number of occasions.)

Meanwhile, things were not going well at the Quaker church formerly pastored by Wimber, which he and his wife Carol were still attending. This situation greatly troubled Carol, who was a member of the church board. She later wrote a detailed article describing this time. According to her account, in September, 1976 she had a disturbing dream, which suggested that she had been wrong in her strong opposition to the charismatic movement. She resigned from the church board and spent three weeks in intensive self-examination and prayer. Out of this, she experienced a powerful personal spiritual renewal and became convinced that God was about to do something new and important in the church.[9]

In October, 1976 a few leaders in the Quaker congregation started a home meeting to encourage one another in their teaching ministries. The meeting grew from twelve to fifty people and began attracting some who had been away from the church for years. Carol attended from the beginning, and John joined the group in January, 1977. The group mushroomed to 125, and the congregation eventually asked the group to leave the church. The group asked for and received a letter of dismissal and blessing, but that experience seems to have had a profound effect on Wimber's views of revival in relation to the established church. On Mother's Day, May 8, 1977, the group, now numbering 150, began meeting as a separate church called Calvary Chapel—Yorba Linda. Wimber preached on the reputation of illegitimacy that followed Jesus throughout his earthly life and argued that the breakaway church, born of the Spirit, would carry that stigma also. From that time on, Wimber began to see the established church as resistant to revival and to believe in the necessity of starting something new.

In 1978 Wimber left Fuller and began to pastor the new church full-time. He preached on Luke, stressing the healings and exorcisms of Jesus, and prayed earnestly and unceasingly for healings in his church. Finally, after ten months, one woman was healed of a fever. Wimber left her house and shouted, "We got one!"[10]

The congregation soon experienced more healings and charismatic manifestations. Many non-Christians were attracted and became Christians. Among them, apparently, was well-known folk singer Bob Dylan, who had been moving toward a Christian worldview for several years. Dylan fit well into Vineyard's non-traditional milieu, with its prophetic critique of the establishment and strong emphasis on vigorous, rock-style music. Dylan's conversion and the new direction in the content of his songs became a sensation in the music world. His Christianity was celebrated in a book by Don Williams, a Presbyterian minister who is now a staunch advocate of the Vineyard movement.[11] Dylan, however, now seems to have left the Vineyard and Christianity and gone in search of his Jewish roots.

The Vineyard congregation continued to move deeper into charismatic phenomena. Mother's Day, 1981 marked the start of "power evangelism." Wimber had asked a young member of the church to preach. After giving his testimony, the young man called all the young people forward. They began shaking, speaking in tongues and falling on the ground. John was evidently concerned about the excessive emotionalism. According to Carol, he prayed all night asking if the phenomena were from God. Early in the morning a friend phoned with a message from God: "It's Me."[12]

The congregation then numbered 700; the average age was 19. By 1982 the average age had risen to 21. In May, 1982 the church changed its name to "Vineyard" in order to identify with Kenn Gulliksen and his seven Vineyards. In September, 1983 it relocated to Anaheim, California. By 1985 the congregation had grown to 5000 members and another 120 Vineyard congregations had been founded. Many of these were already established independent congregations or congregations belonging to another denomination which joined the Vineyard bandwagon in the expectation of experiencing revival. Often, it was the pastors who led their churches into the Vineyard fold after having experienced a Wimber seminar.

Signs and Wonders Seminars

In 1981 Peter Wagner, newly installed in the chair of church growth at Fuller Theological Seminary, asked John Wimber to teach a course in the School of World Mission on the way in which miraculous works had led to rapid evangelization on the mission field. The course (MC510, "Signs and Wonders and Church Growth") soon became one of the most popular and controversial courses at Fuller. (It should be noted, however, that enrollment in the course was swelled by a considerable number of young people from Wimber's own church, who took no other courses at the Seminary.) Wimber would lecture and then hold a workshop in which students were taught and encouraged to pray for healings and later to practise exorcisms. The editor of *Christian Life* was invited to attend the course, and within a month a whole issue of that magazine (October, 1982) was devoted to the subject. Well-known Christian psychologist and author John White took the course in 1984 and has since become a committed Wimber follower, although he differs with Wimber on how to interpret some aspects of the movement.[13] On the other hand, MC510 was achieving a notoriety that troubled other members of the Fuller community. Contrary to later claims,[14] the course had never had unanimous support within the School of World Mission. For instance, while Wimber widely quoted Paul Hiebert in his course materials, he used some of Hiebert's basic assumptions to reach widely different conclusions. Hiebert and other professors in the School of World Mission and the School of Theology began to raise questions about the biblical and theological bases for the course. Some critics were concerned about Wimber's lack of academic credentials. Others felt that healings should occur in the context of the church rather than in a school. Other professors in both the School of World Mission and the School of Theology defended the course. The issue threatened to cause division in the Seminary, in which for many years charismatics and noncharismatics had lived in harmony. In 1985 the Seminary put the course on hold and appointed a study commission to examine the issue. This commission published its findings in 1987.[15] The course was restructured, with various Fuller faculty (but not John Wimber) lecturing. The workshops were canceled, but students were encouraged to observe healings and other miraculous works in various church settings, including Wimber's.

Wimber meanwhile took his course on the road. He has now

presented it and other seminars throughout the United States and Canada and in Ireland, the United Kingdom, Sweden, Germany, South Africa, New Zealand and Australia.

Typical, perhaps, is Wimber's impact on the Lower Mainland area of the Canadian province of British Columbia. In May, 1985 Wimber presented his "Signs and Wonders" seminar to 2300 participants in conjunction with the Burnaby Christian Fellowship, one of the leading independent charismatic churches in the area. The seminar was supported by a number of pastors and congregations of many denominations. A year later another seminar, "Teach us to pray," was held, attracting over 2000 people. Participants were charged $150 for the first seminar and $95 for the second. Shortly after the second seminar, a number of Vineyard fellowships were planted in the area, incorporating many of the people who had attended the seminars and even swallowing up whole congregations. One of the new congregations is in North Delta, B.C., where Ken Blue is pastor and psychologist John White is associate pastor. Both men have become important leaders in the Vineyard movement and have written extensively on its theology.[16]

John Wimber's traveling seminars have been followed up by a number of publishing efforts, in which Wimber was assisted by Kevin Springer. In 1985 they published a book called *Power Evangelism.*[17] This was quickly followed up by a second book, *Power Healing.*[18] These books, along with a variety of tapes, cassettes, songbooks and worship aids, are marketed through Vineyard Ministries International, an entity established in 1982 to schedule and promote seminars by Wimber and a number of associates.[19] These materials, dates, and locations of seminars and other information are offered to non-Vineyard churches and Christians through a 16-page magazine, *Equipping the Saints* (originally called *First Fruits*), edited by Suzanne Springer. Another periodical, *Worship Update*, is aimed at worship leaders and church musicians.

Although Wimber said at first that he had no intention of starting another denomination, in 1986 the Association of Vineyard Churches was establshed. The denomination has its own periodical, *The Vineyard Newsletter*, edited by Suzanne Springer. The work of the churches is supervised by national and regional pastoral coordinators.[20] Missionaries have been sent out to the third world. By 1987 there were over 200 Vineyard fellowships in North America alone. Wimber currently aims to have over 10,000 members in his Anaheim congregation (double the present number), and the association hopes to plant up to 10,000 Vineyards "in the coming decades."[21]

(In preparing this book, we invited a number of people to describe their varied experiences with the Vineyard movement. These are the responses. Out of sensitivity to delicate local church situations, we have chosen to carry these pieces anonymously.)

My experience with the Vineyard movement began with a trip to the city of Los Angeles. It was a seminary class field trip, and John Wimber was one of the many pastors we were planning to interview. I remember being very impressed with Wimber's vision for outreach, worship and nurture. I wasn't very impressed with his rather autocratic leadership style.

I next came into contact with the Vineyard movement four years later. I was, and am, pastoring a rural Canadian church. A fellow minister invited me to a "healing seminar," then, a year later, to a "worship seminar."

Both seminars were well attended by people from a broad spectrum of denominational backgrounds. I very much appreciated the freedom I felt to worship with the others in the manner with which I was comfortable. Some stood. Others sat or kneeled. With eyes closed or open, hands raised or folded, we experienced the presence of God in our worship. Despite our differences, we were all disciples of the one Lord, Jesus Christ.

I was afraid of excessive emotionalism at the seminars. Although some people did get out of hand, the emotional pitch did not ever come close to that of a football game, for example. Actually, the seminar leaders from Vineyard Ministries explicitly discouraged excessive emotionalism. Interestingly, the normal "low" that I feel after an emotional "high" didn't happen after the Vineyard seminars.

I must admit I went suspicious that the Vineyard people were proselytizing. However, I felt no attempts to proselytize. In fact, I felt very strongly that Vineyard's purpose in doing the seminars was to equip us to minister more effectively in our home churches. That is what has happened. My own walk with God has been deepened and enriched. My ministry as a pastor has also become more effective. Overall, I have had a positive, upbuilding experience with Vineyard Ministries.

• • • • •

My wife and I were both brought up in very stable Christian homes and are deeply grateful for a solid Bible foundation.

In coming to the Vineyard, we have become intimate with God through worship. When we have a time of worship in singing each Sunday morning, we enter into the presence of God by singing songs of worship directly to the King of Kings, my Abba Father. I feel like I can bring my praise and worship directly to my heavenly Father and in response my Father lovingly puts his arms around me and says, "I love you, my child!" I have found a vast difference between singing hymns *about* God and singing songs of praise that express our deepest feeling of love directly *to* God.

In my one and a half years at the Vineyard, I am extremely pleased at how often the leaders have stressed that we as Christians are all a part of the body of Christ. We may have small differences from one denomination to the next, but these should not cause us to judge that group of believers and consider ourselves as more favored by God. It's time we stop shooting at each other. We need to turn around and realize who the real enemy is (Satan). We as Christians need to stand united against the enemy so we can push back the forces of darkness and shine the light of Jesus.

I came to the Vineyard with some deep inner hurts and also some sinful practices which I could not overcome. At first I was hesitant to open up to anyone because, in the church I came from, it was unheard of to let anyone know that you did not have it all together. Within four months, my home group leaders and other members had shown me so much love and acceptance that I trusted them and could share my hurts and struggles. In my late teens (I'm now 34) there was a suicide in my family, and all the trauma that this had caused me now came to the surface and needed to be dealt with. I received relief from the shame and release from all the feelings of deep inner hurt. It was like a giant burden lifted off my back.

Since coming to the Vineyard, we have received much excellent training through seminars, training sessions and Sunday morning messages. But the more we learn and understand about our heavenly Father, the more we realize that we are only beginning to catch a glimpse of how he is preparing and purifying his body of believers. All we as believers need to do is earnestly seek him with all our hearts.

• • • • •

I have been brought up to believe that God is essentially in favor of healing and that he can work through us as his instruments, but I have witnessed very little in terms of an aggressive seeking after God with respect to the restoration of the physically afflicted. There is a marked difference between what I have observed in the church and the experience of the first-century Christian community. Only through my own experience as a missionary in Madrid, Spain, a context akin to the Athens and Corinth of Paul's time, have I begun to ask myself and my comrades about the validity of advancing the kingdom of God through a salvation message more holistic and practical in its approach.

I concur at points with some criticisms of "Signs and Wonders," especially those relating to the sensationalism and "hyping" allegedly associated with the healing conferences. I too found myself a bit uneasy at a recent Wimber conference in Dublin, Ireland titled "Healing in the Church." On the other hand, I am grateful for a spirit of openness and increasing participation in praying for the sick, but with caution, discernment and the blessing of the church community. Too often, perhaps, we as Christians have been guilty of wrongfully encouraging the sick to "persevere" when God so much desired us to authoritatively say, "Stand up and walk!"

Recently it was our opportunity to minister to a family whose young son is suffering from a serious paralytic condition. Ironically, several days after our visit, another friend of this family was wanting to "minister" to them through the curative and mystic powers of a local "healer." If we as Christians are not open to serving the suffering through the love of Christ and in the power and discernment of the Spirit, we just may be missing God's holistic touch—at the cost of Satan providing his own solution.

● ● ● ● ●

I believe that John Wimber has been used as a catalyst under God to stir into flame embers of renewal that may have been dormant too long. Through the two seminars I attended ("Signs and Wonders" and "Teach us to Pray"), we were given tools to implement many of the things we already knew.

There has been a lot of debate about John Wimber and his theology, but I have not sensed any serious deviation. On the contrary, his emphasis on the supernatural power of God is a reminder of the church's deviation from that with which God would rightfully endow her.

In terms of the Vineyard churches, however, on the basis of what I have heard and personally observed, I have several areas of concern. One is an apparent reaction to former standards, such as the singing of hymns, which are totally ignored, it seems. Also, there seems to be a neglect of the Word at times, with too much emphasis then on experience. Also there seems to be a reaction in dress at times; I have seen a pastor preach in jeans, which didn't particularly impress me! In spite of these criticisms, I wish them well and believe they are exemplary in their missionary zeal and in their thrust to present a gospel that does not only preach a verbal message but also reaches out in areas of healing and deliverance.

● ● ● ● ●

Thank you for asking for my response and experiences with John Wimber's activities. I have done extensive research (many, many hours), but I'm sure you have all that information. So, I'll just voice a deep concern that I have. I have prayed, "Lord, help me not to be critical, but please also help me not to be gullible." My concern is for our pastors and leaders who are totally gullible and do not see the doctrinal error and proud attitude of Wimber. Many of our leaders are afraid to be positive and take a stand by hiding behind the biblical truth, "lest we find ourselves fighting against God" (Acts 5:39). With the information and the results of a man-centered movement that we have, why don't we take a stand? I am deeply concerned.

• • • • •

On an early Advent Sunday some four or five years ago, the minister at our church preached a sermon on Mary and Elizabeth. Appropriate enough for the forthcoming Christmas season, it would seem. Something about the sermon, however, made me uneasy. Elizabeth, we were told, praised God from the fullness of the Spirit; Mary, however, quoted from the Psalms. While the minister did not lift the one above the other, he did imply clearly enough that the two could be separated. This came after nearly three months of preaching in which virtually every sermon, whether or not the text warranted it, was used to emphasize the work of the Holy Spirit. Had there been some evidence of the power of the Spirit to go with the words, the effect might have been different. There was none, however; they remained words without effect.

In the meantime, the minister began to sense that he was losing control of the situation. Never an outstanding orator—he was inexperienced in pastoral work when he came—he had made the mistake early on of extending his sermons from half an hour to forty-five minutes. Rather than give him more time to develop his sermons, the extra time merely helped to accentuate his oratorical and exegetical weaknesses. People began to leave the church—as they do in evangelical circles when things go against their expectations. His response was to try to get control of every committee in the church and to chastise the congregation into submission from the pulpit.

It was not long thereafter that he preached on discipleship. The sermon was a disaster, as negative a sermon as I have ever heard. He was clearly ill at ease with the whole concept, and ended by calling it a "real bummer." He tried to salvage the wreckage by concluding that only with the help of the Holy Spirit could this high calling be fulfilled.

Well before this happened, the pastor, associate pastor and some members of the congregation had begun to attend Wimber's seminars in Los Angeles. Not only were these the source of the pastor's new-found emphasis on the Holy Spirit, but the fact that he, from the pulpit, called Wimber a new prophet signified that he believed new revelations to be coming from Wimber. Some of the group, with deep psychological problems, became involved with inner healing and Wimber's other extra-biblical procedures. The new authoritarianism must also have had its source in Wimber, as did the group's desire to experience the "spectacular gifts." "Mood music" entered the Sunday morning worship service, music to put us into the proper frame of mind to be able to "experience" the Spirit. An emphasis on the spiritual gifts became pervasive at the same time that discipleship was called a "real bummer." "Intellectuals" were administered a real drubbing on one occasion by a pastoral intern who had just alienated the young people and destroyed the youth program in the process.

Eventually, at the instigation of one of the members, a meeting of some of the disaffected was held. The group then requested a meeting with the pastor and the board of elders. It was a meeting where candor reigned. Both the pastor and the board were clearly taken aback, especially the board, which appeared quite frankly adrift. One thing led to another until finally the board took a vote of confidence on the pastor. It resulted in an evenly divided verdict. Thereupon, the pastor asked his opponents on the board to resign, but they refused. Eventually, the issue came before the entire congregation. In two congregational meetings, all issues were aired. When it became clear to the board members that the majority of opinion was no longer with the pastor, that in fact his retention would split the congregation in two, his resignation was finally requested. The associate pastor, who had resigned earlier, now wished to be considered for the position of senior pastor, but he was not rehired. In the wake of these decisions, a number of people left the church, many joining the Vineyard movement, while others joined other charismatic groups. About 125 members were left to try to pick up the pieces.

Was this the work of the Holy Spirit? The work of Satan? Or the work of fallible human beings? When the pastor was a candidate, he was asked by a university student what theological books he had read recently and who his favorite theologian was. His answer was a blank on both counts. There was clearly a theological vacuum here waiting to be filled. For various reasons, John Wimber came to fill the vacuum.

• • • • •

I am saddened by what comes across as essentially negative assessments of the Vineyard movement. I react this way because of the blessings I've received at a Vineyard seminar.

In the fall of 1985 I returned from a summer mission assignment in India, having contracted amoebic dysentery. I was extremely sick, and I was seeing the best doctors in the city for treatment. Meanwhile, my church was praying earnestly and consistently for me to be healed. When a Vineyard team came to a nearby church to do a seminar on healing, I attended, with the reservations I feel would probably characterize most of us. At that seminar, the Holy Spirit touched my body and began to heal me of my dysentery. I believe that God answered the prayers of the brothers and sisters in my home church and simply used people from a Vineyard team. The healing was not instantaneous but gradual and definite, having begun at the seminar. When I shared all this with my church, they rejoiced with me in God's goodness.

It is my sincere hope that other Christians would view the Vineyard movement as part of the body of Christ that God is using greatly in a specific area of ministry. God used *both* the prayers of my home church and those of the Vineyard team to bless me in a physical way. May we not all thank God together for his grace, instead of criticizing our fellow brothers and sisters in Christ?

• • • • •

In January, 1983 we moved to a new province. We looked forward to settling down in our new home. One of our concerns was what to do about a church home. We had been quite involved in church work up to this point, and we felt we were ready for a break. We knew only one or two families at our new location. Before we moved, one of these friends called and told us that they were planning to start a new church—would I be willing to get involved in the diaconate? I told him about our previous decision not to be involved. "That's fine," he said. "Take a couple of weeks off, but will you be involved after that?" I said I would. After we moved, I was soon very much a part of the church.

In less than a year we were without a pastor. Some months later a young man came to take his place. Things went quite well. He was a little charismatic maybe, but then a *little* outward action was good, I thought. Then, one evening at our council meeting, our pastor told us about a seminar being held by John Wimber and that all who could should attend. Who is John Wimber, we asked. He is from Fuller Seminary and is speaking mainly to church leaders. Could he go? Permission was granted, and he attended. This was followed by a few more seminars. Before long it became evident that the pastor and the council had different goals in mind. It also became evident that at these seminars the emphasis was on signs and wonders and healing. Then came the videotapes, which were shown to a certain group in the church. After seeing one tape, I could see that very slowly but very surely there was a split coming in our church family. I prayed long and hard for unity, but it did not come. There were people leaving the church.

In the spring we were out of the province for a few weeks. One day a call came, and the voice on the other end said, "It happened. The split has come." My heart sank, and I felt sick. Why, God? How different from the first call I received. I didn't want to ever go back. Who wants to go back to broken pieces? These were part of my family, my friends, whom I had helped along the way and whom I loved. I struggled for weeks. I knew God wanted me to go back, but I didn't want to go. One day I went to see a very good friend for counsel. He said, "You need to go back. One day these same people may need you, so continue to be their friend."

I went back with a heavy heart. The Lord has since given me a new joy in serving him. Some of the same people who left our church have since called and said, "Have you time to listen? Things are not going so good." I praise God for the opportunity to serve. To him be the glory.

Part Two

HISTORICAL CONSIDERATIONS

Adherents of the Vineyard movement (particularly John White in his book *When the Spirit Comes with Power*) have frequently appealed to church history, drawing parallels to previous revivals and suggesting that theirs is the latest in a series of powerful movements brought about by the Holy Spirit.

What is the history of revival in the church? What can we learn from the blessings and the mistakes of the past that can guide us in the present? Four scholars give their answers.

Abraham Friesen

"Unless you people see miraculous signs and wonders," Jesus told him, "you will never believe" (John 4:48). The seminars given by John Wimber are entitled "Signs and Wonders." Wimber, however, uses Hebrews 2:3-4 as his proof-text: "God also testified to it by signs, wonders and various miracles, and gifts of the Holy Spirit distributed according to his will."

In the first passage, signs and wonders would appear to be the way, or at least one way, in which God testifies to his work, although Jesus here clearly regards them as a concession to the unbelief of the people. But the key to the second passage is the little word "it." "It" refers back to what the King James Version calls "so great (a) salvation." God's *salvation* was attested to by signs and wonders, and that at a very specific time in salvation history. The passage says nothing about signs and wonders in the present.

One of Wimber's supporters has stated bluntly, "We want the spectacular gifts." Precisely this attitude was castigated by Jesus in John 4:48. When signs and wonders occur, God uses them for his purposes, not ours. And the passage in Hebrews 2 clearly refers to Christ's coming and the salvation he wrought as the event to which God testified with signs and wonders.

The above is but one small example of a disconcerting tendency within the movement begun by John Wimber to manipulate the meaning of scripture for one's own "higher" purposes. This is a tendency that is all too often combined with a claim to personal inspiration and infallibility. Such a combination is not accidental. The claim to personal inspiration and infallibility invariably leads one to "adjust" or "reinterpret" the scriptures to conform with one's own "inspired" position. According to Roberta Hestenes, a professor at Fuller Theological Seminary, Wimber once claimed "virtual infallibility" in her presence.[1] In contrast, even Christ, when tempted by Satan, responded by pointing to the written Word of God, saying repeatedly, "It is written."

The essential problem at the heart of the Wimber phenomenon, therefore, is the problem of the relationship of the written Word to the Holy Spirit. This is not a new problem. In the sixteenth century Martin Luther struggled against Thomas Muentzer, who sought to subordinate the Word to his mystical experience of the Spirit. In opposition, Luther repeatedly asserted the unity of Word and Spirit. The Word was not merely a "testimony" or "witness" to the experience of the Spirit. Any experience, even one of the Spirit, could not be self-authenticating; it needed always to be tested by the revealed Word of God. Not the experience but the Word was the final arbiter of God's truth. John Calvin made the same point when he wrote, "For when they boast extravagantly of the Spirit, the tendency certainly is to sink and bury the Word of God, that they may make room for their own falsehoods."[2]

The Abyss of the Soul

The "extravagant" emphasis on the Holy Spirit, the claim to "virtual infallibility" and the tendency to "bury the Word of God" have their origin in medieval mysticism and the non-Christian sources upon which the mystics drew. Like Thomas Muentzer in the sixteenth century, John Wimber not only cites these mystics with approval, but also manifests the same tendencies.

The mystics, however, knew the non-Christian source of their basic assumption; John Wimber, apparently, does not. That assumption has to do with the nature of the human soul and how it perceives God. In this respect, the mystics spoke of an "abyss" of the soul in which God resides. John Tauler, perhaps the most influential of these medieval mystics, wrote:

> This deepest region of the spirit was in a manner known to some of the Gentiles of old; and as they searched its depths, this knowledge caused them to despise all transitory things. Such great philosophers as Proclus and Plato gave a clear account of it to guide others who knew it not. Therefore, St. Augustine says that Plato proclaimed the first part of St John's gospel (1:1-5) . . . . The same philosopher gained some knowledge of the most holy Trinity. Children, all such things come from the deep recesses of the soul, in which such men as Plato lived and whose stores of wisdom they had access to.[3]

According to this view, the human soul contained what the German mystics called an *Abgrund*, an abyss. Men like Plato and Proclus, both secular Greek philosophers, had access to divine wisdom directly because, as Tauler said, they lived in these "deep recesses of the soul." Although they had never come into contact with the "written Word" or the "Word made flesh," they nevertheless shared its wisdom because they had plumbed the "deep recesses of their souls." Clearly then, truth came from within, not from any external revelation from God.

Tauler was right. This view came directly from Plato, particularly from his *Timaeus*. There Plato spoke of the human soul as the "immortal principle" within man. This soul was akin to the Creator and came to be called the "divine spark" within man. This argument, that one had a divine spark within, came into Christian thought through the Church Fathers. These great thinkers of the early church, beginning with Justin Martyr and culminating in St. Augustine, had nearly all been Platonists before they became Christians. Because of certain similarities, they were attracted to Christianity as a higher form of the same truth that Plato had perceived.[4] Augustine especially in his early years developed the Platonic view of the soul and integrated it into his Christianity.[5] Thus he could say, "The soul has within itself a hidden abyss, and the things of time and this world have no place therein, but only what is high above." It was in this hidden abyss of the soul that God resided. Therefore, one could find God only by turning inward. Following Augustine, Tauler described the soul in these words:

> Of the dignity of the soul . . . many masters, new and old, have treated . . . . Some teachers speak of it as a spark of divine fire, others as the inmost depths of the soul, others again as the crown of the soul, or its origin and the source of life. Albertus, however, calls it an interior image, in which the blessed Trinity is manifested in the soul. This divine spark, say others, flies upward so high in the soul, that the understanding cannot follow it, for it is ever passing again upward into the divine center which is its uncreated source.[6]

For Plato, the "immortal principle" meant that if the soul could be freed from the passions of the flesh through the victory of reason, it could eventually return to its immortal source. Fifteenth and sixteenth-century Renaissance Humanists, imbued with the same Platonic philosophy, argued that man had the power "out of the soul's judgment, to be reborn into the higher forms, which are divine."[7] The humanist position, that man can reach perfection without Christ, therefore has its source in the same ideas that also fed mysticism. Both believed that man has it within him to reach perfection because of his "divine spark."

The Deification of Man

With such a view of the soul, it is not surprising that adherents from Plato to the Renaissance Humanists, from Augustine to the medieval mystics and Thomas Muentzer, can speak of the "deification of man." After all, man has within him a divine spark which, if ignited, can start a holy fire that can purify the individual. Augustine at one point spoke of "growing god-like." Pico della Mirandola, the fifteenth-century Renaissance Humanist, spoke of "being reborn into the higher forms, which are divine." Similarly, the medieval mystics and Thomas Muentzer also spoke of being deified, of reaching god-like perfection while yet in this life.

The mystics, however, spoke of growing god-like with a difference. It was a difference that had to do with the role the Holy

Spirit played in bringing about a "successful" conversion. By the latter they meant the ability to live the perfect Christian life. Tauler spoke of such a "true and entire conversion to God" in a number of places and always in terms of the "descent of the Holy Spirit into a man's soul." This resulted, he said, in the "stirring up with a powerful movement of grace his whole interior life," which so totally transformed him that the things he once loved now became absolutely tasteless to him.[8] Such a conversion could only take place if the rubble heaped upon the human soul had been cleared away, if the "garden of the soul" had been properly weeded, as Tauler put it. Then one had to turn away from all "creatures," all external things, and turn inward to one's soul where God resided. Now the work of transformation could begin, now "the divine birth in the soul of man" could take place.[9] Knowing the external written Word of God was not enough.

Spirit versus Word

From this mystical perspective, Word and Spirit were, at least to a certain extent, in conflict. While the "letter" of the external Word killed, the Spirit made alive. Muentzer, therefore, called Luther a "scribe" (as in "scribes and Pharisees") because he believed him to possess a merely "rational" understanding of the Word. Muentzer, on the other hand, possessed the "living Word," the Holy Spirit within. Tauler had taught him, "All the truth that those teachers who follow reason alone have ever taught, all that such will ever teach till the last day, is nothing in comparison to the wisdom in the depths of the soul."[10] Therefore, Tauler continued, one "should not busy himself overly much with books" but rather "strive after the Spirit of God."[11] This internal Word, this living voice of God, was not dependent upon the written, external Word of God. "You must know," Tauler said, "that the Eternal Word is self-begotten in the soul and that the soul itself, when favored with the Divine generation in it, knows the Eternal Word better than all teachers can describe him."[12] In the preface to Tauler's sermons was a biographical account of what everyone thought was Tauler's conversion until it was proven spurious in the nineteenth century. There Tauler was told after his conversion, "Now thou hast the light of the Holy Ghost, received from the grace of God, and thou hast the holy Scriptures in thee."[13]

The claim to possess the Holy Spirit in such a way as to receive his message undiluted and thus have "the most secret meaning of holy scripture imparted . . . . and the truth of God nakedly revealed" not only makes the Bible superfluous, but it also breeds a kind of anti-intellectualism. In Muentzer's case, it led him to consider biblical scholarship as at best unnecessary. As reflected in the following passage from Tauler's sermons, it makes religious truth purely subjective: "The Holy Spirit is a marvellous workman. To teach everything that he pleases requires no time—a simple touch and all is taught the soul—nothing more is necessary."[14] In like fashion, Thomas Muentzer asserted that he had received everything "directly from the mouth of God."[15]

With this anti-intellectualism comes a type of spiritual arrogance that ill becomes the Christian. If one claims to possess the Holy Spirit and has been inspired by him, and that infallibly, then anyone who disagrees with such a person must at best be a lesser Christian, at worst a servant of the devil. The diligent and careful study of the scripture, by which we might hope to reconcile our differences, is scuttled.

Deluded by Human Influences

While such a position might make us feel spiritually superior to, and critical of, everyone else, it leaves us nakedly exposed to the influences around us. Wimber has insisted that "at some point critical thinking must be laid aside. When are we going to see a generation (which) doesn't try to understand this book (the Bible) but just believes it?" As Don Lewis has pointed out, what Wimber really means is "When are we going to see a generation that believes *my* interpretation?" After all, Wimber's interpretation, inspired by the Holy Spirit, is the only right one. All others, as Thomas Muentzer had also argued, are merely "rational" interpretations, not inspired ones. Like Muentzer's message, Wimber's too has been received "directly from the mouth of God." The problem with Muentzer's message so received is that it led to the disaster of the Peasants' War of 1525. The product of Wimber's message has been, in many places, division and bitterness.

If we look carefully at all the things Muentzer received "directly from the mouth of God," we find the following. He derived his understanding of the soul from Tauler, who knew clearly enough that it came from Greek philosophy. The model for his conversion came from the spurious biography of Tauler. His eschatology came from Augustine's erroneous interpretation of the parable of the tares. And one could go on. What in fact happened to Thomas Muentzer was that when he placed the Holy Spirit above scripture, he lost the one sure criterion by which to judge what his "spirit" was telling him. It was no wonder that his whole world collapsed when he became involved in the Peasants' War of 1525. He had expected that this was "the time of harvest" in which he—in place of the angels spoken of in Matthew 13—would separate the wheat from the tares. Instead, his army of peasants was slaughtered by their opponents. That event, more than anything else, proved that Muentzer had not received his insights "directly from the mouth of God." Instead, because he separated Word from Spirit, he gave opportunity for all kinds of spurious human ideas to influence him. While he could hammer away at the man-made laws and traditions of the Roman Catholic church, he seemed oblivious to the fact that, in the final analysis, he was merely substituting his own in their place.[17] Is John Wimber doing the same?

The Gospel of John begins with the familiar verse: "In the beginning was the Word, and the Word was with God, and the Word was God." It is this Word that is eternal, not our experience of it. When we begin to depart from this "external" standard—no matter how difficult it may be to interpret—we inevitably run into trouble. Our experiences, conditioned by the times in which we live, our personalities, our culture, our positions in life, can never be absolute; they are always relative. That is the essence of being human and finite.

From the basis of experience, Wimber can dabble in Jungian psychology—which itself has mystical roots. He can accept such practices as "visualization," the "healing of memories" and other extra-biblical ideas and practices. He can claim to have discovered the methods by which God's power can be manipulated. In recommending the Linn brothers, the most prominent members of the inner healing movement, Wimber writes, "Father Dennis and Matthew Linn . . . are Jesuit priests who have written books which deal with physical, psychological and spiritual wholeness. They are highly trained in psychology and combine the best insights in this field with theological understanding, shaped by charismatic experience."[18] Not a word about scripture.

When the Catholic church of the Middle Ages began to claim infallibility around the twelfth century, Aristotle and other philosophical "traditions of men" entered its teachings. It was these traditions Luther rejected in 1524 when he wrote, "The gold must be rescued from these men, and the pure scripture separated from their dross and filth." The same holds true for Wimber's teachings.

As soon as we take our eyes off the Bible with its absolute standards, our perspective becomes blurred by the relativity all around us. The gifts of the Holy Spirit become *our* gifts. God's power becomes our power, so that we can manipulate God to meet our needs. And power is the watchword of the Wimber movement. One hears little of servanthood, of discipleship, of carrying one's cross. Indeed, crosses are to be gotten rid of through miraculous cures. We want to see the spectacular. So much is this the case that Wimber confessed to a follower not too long ago that his parishioners were no longer interested in hearing the scripture read and expounded. But in the pursuit of the spectacular, we may well miss God, who came to Elijah in a still, small voice.

It is not John Wimber who has discovered the true meaning and power of the gospel. The Reformation struggle is very instructive here. Wimber, like Thomas Muentzer, points to his experience of the Holy Spirit. Martin Luther points to Christ on the cross. It is in the crucified one that we must place our faith, not in Wimber's experience.

The Power of Pietism

Victor G. Doerksen

Pietism can be traced back to the early seventeenth century, when the popular preacher Johannes Arndt (1555-1621) addressed his *Four Books of True Christianity* to a somewhat cool and formalized Lutheran orthodoxy. His popular sermons were addressed to the hearts of his hearers, and his exhortation was to a warm and active spiritual life rather than to doctrinal purity. Other preachers and hymn writers like Paul Gerhardt (1607-76) joined the effort to restore spiritual vitality to the state churches of the German lands.

Classical Pietism takes its focus from the work of Philip Jacob Spener (1635-1705), whose tract *Pia Desideria*, originally written as a preface to a new edition of Arndt's book in 1675, gave the movement its name. Spener, like Arndt before him, took up impulses from earlier mystical writings, especially the *Theologia Germanica* written by an unknown fourteenth-century mystic. Following the emphases of these writers, Spener addressed the inner life of the Christian: " . . . it is not enough that we hear the Word with our outer ear, but we must let it penetrate to our heart, so that we may hear the Holy Spirit speak there, that is, with vibrant emotion and comfort feel the sealing of the Spirit and the power of the Word."[1] Spener advocated a return to a personal reading of the scriptures and the active priesthood of the believer, who should worship in the temple of his body and not only in the temple of his church. By thus speaking about the inner life of the individual Christian, Spener helped to set in motion a shift in emphasis from the church to the individual and his spiritual story. The Pietism of Spener was Bible-centered and orthodox, but in the groups that formed under his influence there developed tendencies of separation and dispute, which were to become widespread during the later eighteenth and nineteenth centuries.

At the same time, there were also elements of the outward-working piety later taught by August Hermann Francke (1663-1727). While Spener's tract had been addressed to teachers and students of theology, Francke's practical activity was largely in the area of institutions like schools and orphanages. But it was not so much his many acts of charity which were remembered about Francke; rather, it was the autobiographical story of his conversion, which added a new element to the Pietist tradition. This "Conversion Report," written in 1690, became a part of Francke's autobiography. It made several new religious concepts popular: a crisis conversion experience which becomes the center as well as the beginning of one's spiritual journey, and the notion of a spiritual crisis as a necessary precondition of this personal conversion experience. These elements have remained a part of the Pietist-evangelical tradition, though with varying degrees of emphasis.

A Place of Refuge

Apart from all else, it is clear that these emphases led to more subjective and individualized forms of religion. Later, leading figures like Count Nikolaus Zinzendorf (1700-60) and Johann Heinrich Jung-Stilling (1740-1817) explored the individual and subjective aspects of religious experience in a variety of ways, the former primarily in his numerous hymns and poems and the latter in his semi-fictional religious writings.

Zinzendorf applied mystical and pietistic ideas to the music of the church and developed a vocabulary based on the walk of the individual with the Savior. Although some of his songs have become standards of the hymn tradition, his excessive use of love-language and familiar forms of address trivialized religious language. For example, Zinzendorf, following the mystics, gazed upon the wounds of Christ and spoke amorously about the "pretty little hole" in Christ's side where he would find refuge. Such excesses have found their way into much modern religious language.

Jung-Stilling took up the idea of the life and adventure of the Christian soul. Following the example of John Bunyan, he personified human qualities and weaknesses and told a tale of the struggle of the soul on the way to its true homeland. His most popular novel, *Homesickness,* transposes this basic plot into an eschatological landscape and has the hero lead the true believers to the gathering place in the East, the place of refuge, where they await the return of Christ. Jung-Stilling's literal readers took him at his word, and some indeed moved in whole communities to an eastern country, largely unknown to them, to await their salvation.

This expectation of the second coming of Christ was added to the Pietist tradition in southern Germany. The Swabian prelate Johann Albrecht Bengel (1687-1752) published an *Explanation of the Revelation of John,* which was followed by a timetable which calculated the return of Christ as occurring on June 18, 1836 (his book appeared in 1740). Bengel's prediction was to have wide-ranging and far-reaching effects. Small groups both inside and outside the official churches took Bengel's eschatological ideas to heart and made them part of their worship and discussion meetings.

Following the French Revolution of 1789, many religious groups believed that the Enlightenment, combined with the political upheavals of the Revolution, would bring about the end time. France, having thrown off its divinely appointed king, would in due course be taken over by the Antichrist. Certain Bible texts seemed to point to Russia, whose czar was both Christian and secure, as the place of refuge where the return of Christ could be awaited in safety.

These events now began to have drastic consequences as the various groups discussed them and the writings of Bengel and Jung-Stilling. Over a half-century, a number of whole communities and many hundreds of individuals decided to sell their possessions and move to eastern territories. Even those who remained often acted under the influence of these teachings. So, for example, the community of Korntal, believing that the second coming would occur in the year 1836, built its houses of thinner beams than was usual since they would not have to last very long in any case.

Much later in the century several groups of Mennonites in southern Russia were moved by similar impulses to travel eastward into the territories around Samarkand and await the second coming, which had been predicted for around 1879. These groups were under the influence, particularly, of Claas Epp, who, like Bengel, had written commentaries based on his reading of scripture, especially the books of Daniel and Revelation. It was not so much their biblical exegesis which was convincing, as the fact that ultimately men like Epp, Jung-Stilling and Bengel claimed they had received inspiration by the Spirit of God and that this divine voice could not be contradicted.

Strange Paths

One may well ask how the original Pietistic emphasis on the inner life of the individual Christian could lead to such drastic and painful consequences. Certainly there were many Christians who benefited in their religious life as a result of the work of Spener. Certainly there is always a need for revitalization of faith, and the positive contribution of Pietism in nurturing the spiritual life of the individual and the "church within the church" should not be underestimated.

But there are several elements inherent in the movement which were inclined to lead its followers onto strange paths. There is the matter of how the scriptures were to be read, for example. The tendency was toward the individual and his own literal interpretation. The emphasis was more on the heart and the feelings of that individual than on reason, which was suspect. The voice of the scripture and of the Spirit was spoken within the heart, and who was to argue with that voice? When the Jung-Stillings and the Claas Epps outlined their views of scripture and its message, who could contradict them? What had begun with Arndt and Spener as an attempt to revive the church eventually led to dispute, fragmentation and dissolution.

Pastor Eduard Wüst, who was a powerful Pietist preacher both in southern Germany and then in Russia, exemplifies what is both best and worst in historical Pietism. His message was biblical, but very emotional and drastic in its language. He had lost his position in Germany because he insisted on using strong imagery in his sermons. He had on one occasion said that the roadways of hell would be paved with the heads of the clerics of Swabia. His message to the Lutherans and Mennonites of the Ukraine was likewise full of religious feeling and invective. Wüst's work led, among other things, to the beginnings of the Mennonite Brethren Church in 1860. As historian P.M. Friesen observed, Wüst brought warmth into the house of Menno but that fervent fire was not without dangerous sparks. Although there is no doubt about beneficial effects in his ministry, it is also unfortunately true that his work caused great friction within the various congregations and led to splinter groups which quarreled bitterly. What began as ardent and sincere piety became a harmful force when allowed to move away from the guiding principles of brotherhood and service. In the last analysis Wüst had brought not peace but a sword, and he died a bitterly disappointed man.

By the middle of the nineteenth century, Pietism was still at work in very different parts of the European Christian world. It was the inner religion of the conservative upper classes, of the Prussian nobility and the factory owners. At the same time, it was a motivating force in the social experiments of Gustav Werner in southern Germany, who founded a self-sustaining community among the destitute of society, and in the teachings of father and son Blumhardt of Bad Boll, whose endeavors led from a teaching and healing ministry of great effect to the founding of the Social Democratic Party of Germany. But most of all, the legacy of Pietism was the continental reawakening, which in its vigorous Methodist preaching and its international missionary outreach, was to lay the foundations for the evangelical Christianity of the twentieth century.

We thus owe much to the tradition of Pietism, which reminded western Christianity that its faith was a matter of the heart and of personal commitment. But there are lessons in its history that may serve as a warning as well.[2]

The Role of Emotions
in Christian Faith

Levi Keidel

It is Sunday morning in a Zairian village. I am participating in the regular worship service of a Mennonite congregation. The neat, mud-walled, thatch-roofed church is packed. I sit squeezed between black people on one of the sturdy bench pews fabricated from local bamboo. The air is charged with expectation.

The song leader takes his position beside the pulpit and calls out a number. A portable foot-pump, legacy of some past missionary, wheezes an opening chord. We stand. Voices sing lustily. Hands clap the beat. Bodies sway in rhythm. Enthusiasm runs high for all five verses. We sit down.

The choir stands. It begins singing an original composition narrating how Jesus raised Lazarus from the dead. Two men enter carrying on a low rack a "dead" person in graveclothes. "Jesus" steps out of the choir. He gestures a shout. The dead arises. Graveclothes tumble to the ground.

The lay pastor announces the offering. The congregation begins clapping and singing the song regularly used for the occasion. Each succeeding verse exhorts a group of the congregation to give. Now it's the women's turn. They reverently emerge from the pews, form a line in each aisle and, in a slow, graceful, dance-like gait, proceed to the front. Each woman curtsies before the communion table and drops her money into the offering basket.

I sit taking it all in. There is no question about it. This is authentic, joyous worship. How can I reconcile this with what I saw at that home prayer meeting last night? The joined living-dining room area was packed. People sat on the floor. Others stood lining the walls. With loud, raised voices all were praying at once. Some were making strange guttural sounds. Someone shrieked. Some heads shook so violently they appeared as a blur. To me, it was bedlam that made concentration upon prayer impossible. Was that authentic?

Emotions in Past Revivals

What is the role of emotions in Christian experience? A reading of the Old Testament makes clear that emotions played an important role in the worship of the Hebrews. They laughed; they danced; they wept; they shouted; they clapped; they raised their hands heavenward—all as a part of their worship of the Lord.

It is normal that people express the presence of the Holy Spirit by reacting emotionally. While the value of nonrational manifestations may be debated, extreme forms of emotional expression have been a part of most of the great revival movements of the past. Anabaptists spoke in tongues, had visions, prophesied and fell into comas.[1] During the New England "Great Awakening" the ministry of Jonathan Edwards produced tremblings, shriekings, convulsions and faintings. Soon John Wesley in England expressed "profound thankfulness" that such "wonderful bodily effects" had become a part of his own ministry.[2] About a century later, faintings and prostrations were a common occurrence under the ministry of American evangelist Charles G. Finney. He believed that the phenomena were "a case of falling under the power of God, as the Methodists would express it."[3]

The historic Cane Ridge, Kentucky revival in 1801-02 was marked by such phenomena. Shrieking in agony, hysterical laughing, barking, leaping and bounding, prolonged body jerking and collapsing into comas were common.[4] Similar occurrences were a part of the British Isles revivals in the mid-nineteenth century and after the turn of the twentieth; the Jamaican revival of 1860; and the East

African revival which began in 1936.

These many examples would suggest that the human psyche may automatically respond in such ways to the sudden impact of Spirit power. But the ongoing manifestation of such signs has almost always proven counterproductive. The above noted great revivalists had a change of heart about the value of such signs. Jonathan Edwards expressed his disenchantment in a published treatise. Persons of his parish manifesting such excesses not only failed to improve their conduct; ultimately, they became hardened of heart and drove him from his pastorate.[5] John Wesley's ardor for such "signs and wonders" waned as he observed their abuse beyond his control; by the time of his death, he felt it was Satan who pushed people to such "extravagance."[6] In his later years, Charles G. Finney came to view his earlier ministry when the fainting manifestations were most prominent as a period of failure. In 1836 Finney said that of all the converts of the revivals of the preceding ten years, "the great body of them are a disgrace to religion."[7]

More recently, a Catholic priest was "slain by the Spirit" (the term used to describe lapsing into a coma). He began incorporating it into his ministry. While initially he gained spectacular popularity, the reactions of some persons began troubling him. Occurrences began to happen involuntarily, as when he walked into a room. On occasions the experience produced hysteria, fear and even terror. Persons would return again and again for a momentary "high" but showed no growth in their Christian lives. He abandoned the practice.[8] When nonrational phenomena undermine the good effects of genuine revival and fail to produce personal edification, their source must be seen as evil.

Sometimes stress produced by religious experience overpowers one's normal ethical restraints. Four of eight evangelists inspired by Finney were forced out of the ministry for sexual immorality.[9] Sexual licentiousness and drunkenness were an early part of the Cane Ridge revival, although it cannot be proven that such excesses were the consequence of persons' religious emotions.[10]

As a more recent example, TV evangelist Oral Roberts, under great emotional stress, announced that, in effect, God held him hostage under threat of death, pending payment by Roberts' viewers of a $4.5 million ransom by a set deadline.

The Role of Emotions

The common experience of the earlier mentioned revivalists would indicate that feelings or emotions in themselves should play no role in validating the rightness or wrongness of one's Christian faith. William James, though a non-Christian himself, would agree with them. James, a pioneer psychologist, published his lifelong findings in 1902 in a book titled *The Varieties of Religious Experience.* He suggested that the person having a profound conversion experience into *any* religion passes through a sequence of six emotional states. He defined them as (1) a period of growing despair, culminating in (2) an encounter with the divine, followed by (3) a great sense of peace and well-being, (4) a sudden perceiving of truth hitherto unrecognized, (5) the appearance that the world itself has undergone a positive change, and (6) the ecstasy of happiness.[11]

Someone is saying, "Those are precisely the feelings I experienced when I became a Christian. Are you saying that they are not valid? Didn't Jesus say that the person who does his will shall *know* his is the way of truth (John 7:17)? Did not the apostle Paul say that the mark of genuine Christian experience is the witness of the Holy Spirit within our hearts responding to God as Father (Romans 8:14-15)?"

I agree. However, a problem comes when emotions alone are used as the criteria for deciding what is right or wrong, when emotions of themselves become my final authority. The problem is well illustrated today by the consensus in secular society which asks, "How can it be wrong when it feels so good?" When we put faith in sensory responses alone, we are in peril. Satan can imitate anything in the sensory realm and thereby leads many astray.

True Christians have always claimed to live not under the lordship of emotions but under the lordship of Christ. During the earliest centuries of church history and ever since the Reformation, the Word, both living and written, has been the final authority in the church's life and practice. The Word is the primary and essential criterion for deciding what is right and wrong. First of all Jesus calls us to obedience. His indwelling presence in us is contingent upon our obedience (John 14:23). When we respond by submitting ourselves to him in our innermost depths, whatever emotions follow are to be welcomed, affirmed and enjoyed.

The prayer meeting described earlier is atypical among the Zairians. I have worshiped with them for 25 years. However, they are closer to the Hebrews than we are. They dance, weep, shout, clap, raise their hands—all in authentic worship. We need not endorse disorderly excesses. Notwithstanding, I recall occasional worship services in Zaire where it seemed the roof alone kept us from ascending into heaven. Such Christians have something to teach us about the role emotions should play in our enjoyment of the Christian faith.

An Historian's Assessment

Donald M. Lewis

The intention of this article is to reflect upon my own experience involving one of John Wimber's conferences, rather than to critique what he has written (although I have read his books). My aim is to evaluate one such gathering from the vantage point of an observer-participant. I was invited to attend a Wimber conference in May of 1985 in my role as a faculty member at Regent College in Vancouver. At that time John Wimber and a team of over one hundred people from his Vineyard Fellowship in California led a four-day seminar entitled "Signs and Wonders and Church Growth." It attracted over 2300 participants, most of whom paid $150 for the opportunity to hear Wimber teach a popularized version of a course which he had previously taught at Fuller Seminary. His enthusiastic local promoters have had him back several times since. Wimber is clearly becoming one of the "hottest items" on the charismatic circuit. He attempts to appeal to a much broader cross section of evangelicals than one might expect. How is one to assess this phenomenon?

Everyone assesses and evaluates from his own standpoint and comes at questions with his own "pre-understanding." I lay my own on the table at the outset. Although I attend an Anglican (Episcopal) church, I was raised in the Pentecostal Assemblies of

Canada (the sister denomination of the Assemblies of God in the USA). I remain sympathetic to the charismatic movement although not actively engaged in it.

Affirmations

Having attended one of Wimber's conferences, there are a number of positive things which I can gladly affirm. Certainly evangelicals should rejoice that the work of the Holy Spirit is being given prominence. Speaking as a church historian, I find it lamentable that the church has often tended to overreact to the excesses of those who have emphasized the Holy Spirit (such as the second-century Montanists, the "left wing" groups among the seventeenth-century Puritans and twentieth-century Pentcostals). What Wimber is doing in drawing attention to the work of the Holy Spirit is a good and helpful thing.

Secondly, his concern to equip believers for ministry is excellent. He wants to see individuals moving out in faith and trusting God to work in new and exciting ways. He is clearly picking up some of the emphases of the "body-life" movement (often associated in people's minds with Ray Stedman of Peninsula Bible Church in California), which has done much in evangelical circles to highlight the need for the "equipping of the saints for the work of the ministry" (Ephesians 4). In this regard, Wimber has a strong emphasis upon the organic nature of the church and urges all of its members to develop their own gifts in ministry.

Thirdly, Wimber offers a good critique of traditional Pentecostal theology and does not formulate his interpretation of personal spiritual renewal in terms of a "second blessing" characterized by speaking in tongues. Here he seems to be relying on George Ladd from Fuller Seminary and upon the English theologian James Dunn.

Fourthly, his vision is for the use of spiritual gifts (such as healing) in terms of evangelism and church growth. He regales his audience with story after story of how the manifestations of miraculous gifts have led to conversions and to the growth of the church.

Fifthly, Wimber has a strong appreciation of "spiritual warfare" and underlines the power of God to combat the forces of darkness.

Sixthly, when it comes to healing, he is careful to reject the teaching of some charismatics and some holiness people who maintain that physical healing is in the atonement—that God has provided for the physical healing of Christians in the sacrifice of his Son.[1] Furthermore, he admits candidly that many of those for whom he has prayed have not been healed. He strongly encourages those who feel that they may have been cured to have a doctor confirm the fact before they go off any medication or suspend treatment. Would that others like him gave the same advice!

Finally, it was delightful to see how encouraged and enthusiastic the vast majority of those who heard Wimber were. Many pastors and lay people were strengthened in their faith and challenged to trust God for greater things in the future. It is clear that his ministry has brought about the spiritual renewal of many Christians and has (humanly speaking) been the means of the conversion of others. In this all Christians should rejoice.

Concerns

If such is the case, need any more be said? Yes indeed, more needs to be said. While rejoicing in the positive aspects of the conference and of Wimber's ministry, I must mention the concerns which some, if not many, evangelicals might have in regard to his emphases. In the first place, the advertising for the conference was rather sensational and left questions about its integrity. The focus was clearly on "signs and wonders," which virtually became an advertising slogan in Wimber's literature. There was a great deal of "hype," not only in the conference brochure but also on the first day of the seminar. Initially Wimber gave the impression that it is commonplace for non-Christians attending his church in Yorba Linda, California, to be converted one day and on the following day to be out on the street casting out demons and healing the sick without even knowing John 3:16 (Wimber's illustration, not mine). Yet on the second day there was almost a complete reversal of emphasis. Things now seemed not to be as simple as first suggested. Wimber began to acknowledge that they see many who are not healed and that some people for whom they pray die rather than recover. Some would see this as Wimber seeking to be balanced. Others see this as inconsistency.

Secondly, one might well ask whether the strong focus upon "signs and wonders" is entirely biblical. Hebrews 2:3-4 is cited as a proof-text: "God also testified to it by signs, wonders and various miracles, and gifts of the Holy Spirit distributed according to his will." But the text indicates that the primary focus is to be upon the gospel: Christians are to be concerned with its proclamation first and foremost. The miraculous signs were sometimes used to draw people's attention to the gospel, that is, to win a hearing for a message which might otherwise have been ignored. At other times they were used to confirm the gospel which had been proclaimed. It is essential to keep in mind that it is the gospel which meets the real needs of men and women; signs and wonders are secondary.

Is there not a danger of becoming sidetracked by sensationalism? The peculiar thing about Jesus' ministry is that he regularly withdrew from the crowds who pursued him because of his reputation as a healer and worker of wonders. Jesus seems constantly to play down the value of "signs and wonders" in terms of attracting a crowd. Perhaps he knew how fickle people were and was only too aware that they often followed him for the wrong reasons. An over-concern with miraculous signs reminds one of Augustine's comment: "Jesus is usually sought for something else, not for his own sake."

A third aspect of the conference which was rather regretful was the strong anti-intellectualism which Wimber exhibited from time to time. It seems to me that on this score he is much more guarded in his writing than he is in person. His insistence that "at some point critical thinking must be laid aside" is nothing less than dangerous. Several times he equated critical thinking with unbelief, and his apparent inability to distinguish between the two is most disturbing. At one point he asked, "When are we going to see a generation (which) doesn't try to understand this book (the Bible) but just believes it?" It seemed that he was asking, "When are we going to see a generation that believes my interpretation of this book without question?" This strong anti-intellectual strain which shows through in Wimber is typical of nineteenth century American revivalism and is just the sort of thing that evangelicalism has been trying to live down in the twentieth century. It disparages God's gracious gift of our minds and reflects ill on a Creator who chose to endow us with the ability to think critically. In his book *Power Evangelism* Wimber is much more careful, but at times he evidences the same bias. In making one point he argues, "First-century Semites did not argue from a premise to a conclusion; they were not controlled by rationalism."[2] It seems that Wimber confuses rationalism and rational thinking. (The former is a view of the world which excludes the supernatural, while rational thinking is defined in the dictionary as "agreeable with reason" and "sane.") Surely Paul's Epistle to the Romans is eminently rational in its argumentation, yet Paul could never be accused of being a rationalist.

While Wimber seemed at times to disparage the intellect, he also attempted to use intellectual argument to convince his listeners of his case. In a lecture on "worldviews," Wimber sought to argue that the western "worldview" is the product of Platonic dualistic thinking, first introduced into western theology by Augustine. Its growing acceptance "during the seventeenth and eighteenth centuries" caused "a new science based on materialistic naturalism" to emerge, which resulted in a "secularization of science and a mystification of religion."[3] Wimber seems to have little appreciation that throughout the centuries Christians have struggled with these questions; for most in his audience, this grossly simplified explanation is enough.

There was no acknowledgement of the extent to which western thinking is rooted in a biblical understanding. At this point we need to ask if Wimber has given serious thought to how other "worldviews" have affected his own, particularly the methodology of healing. In the seminar on healing, one of the phenomena we were instructed to look for was "hot-spots," a buzzword in the New Age thinking emerging in California, which has a hearty blend of Oriental mysticism and Eastern religion.

Theological Concerns

One theological concern arises from Wimber's teaching on healing. People were taught a theology of healing largely based on the observation of phenomenological responses (shaking, stiffening, respiration, laughter, fluttering of eyelids, etc.) and were encouraged to use such subjective criteria to evaluate spiritual responses. The wisdom of someone like Jonathan Edwards, who observed many similar physical responses in the Great Awakening in New England in the 1730s and 1740s, would urge us to be cautious here. The work of the Spirit is seen clearly in the transformation of the lives of sinners, in an increased regard for scripture and in the exaltation of the Savior. Physical and emotional responses are an unreliable basis for the evaluation of a work of God.

A second theological difficulty is Wimber's radical Arminianism. He seems to have little or no appreciation for the doctrine of the fall and speaks of his ministry in terms of "restoring the Edenic state." Has he any real place for an ongoing struggle with the old nature in the life of a Christian, which the New Testament teaches the believer to expect? Will such a view not lead to disillusionment (when the promised state is not attained) or to a refusal to face reality by denying one's own experience of temptation and sin?

Related to this strong emphasis on man's ability is Wimber's view of God's inability. Wimber insists that God often does not get his way in this world, that God's will is regularly thwarted. Here we may well question his doctrine of God. On this point the recent observations by my colleague J.I. Packer are significant. Countering Wimber's views, Dr. Packer has argued that

> my God is not frustrated by any failure on man's part (as Wimber suggests). I think that is the Bible's view of God: He is a sovereign God; he does whatever he pleases . . . . God works out all things according to his own will (Ephesians 1:11). God does whatever he pleases (Psalm 135). And if you are going to lose sight of that aspect of the matter, well then, your doctrine of God is out of shape.[4]

A third area of theological difficulty is Wimber's demonology. Certainly many evangelicals would disagree with his assertion that a Christian can be "demonized." His view seems to contradict the assurance of scripture that "if any man be in Christ he is a new creation, behold old things are passed away, and all things are become new" (II Cor. 5:17). His concern with demonic activity does not seem to take seriously the scriptural injunction that when Christians are afflicted by powers of darkness, they are to "resist the devil," with the assurance that "he will flee from you" (James 4:7).

Another serious objection to Wimber's approach has been raised by Dr. Packer. He sees a danger in that Wimber's ministry encourages anyone suffering from illness always to expect and only to be satisfied with physical healing. Packer feels that such a view does not make allowance for God to use physical suffering as a means of spiritual maturing. In other words, Wimber's approach leaves no room for sanctification through suffering. People need to be reminded, says Packer, that

> there is a special sanctifying value in suffering that is patiently borne with the Lord's help . . . . If you are not careful at this point, prayer for signs and wonders becomes very similar to magic; you are trying to manipulate God. You think you have a way of doing it. You have a magical technique for making him do what you want. But real prayer is built around the thought of "Thy will be done" and, what the person praying ought to be trying to do is to get into the will of God rather than to persuade God to do (what the person wants done).[5]

Two other aspects of Wimber's theology seem to be closely linked: his eschatology (doctrine of last things) and his ecclesiology (doctrine of the church). John Wimber has a love-hate relationship with the church. He professes to love it in all of its expressions and is strong in his denunciations of divisions within it. Almost in the same breath, however, he is devastating in his criticisms: "The church has become wicked in its pride and separation;" "The church is an unbelieving and perverse generation today." Wimber, frequently cynical and disparaging in his references to other churches (including churches which emphasize Bible study and even churches which major on the charismatic gifts), has compared the present state of the church to the relationship between David and Bathsheba.

None of these devastating criticisms are applied to Wimber's own Vineyard Fellowship, however. In his view, Christ is now purifying the church, and Wimber's fellowship is in the vanguard of this work. Here his understanding of the last days began to shine through. Wimber stated categorically that he did not believe in the imminent return of Christ for the church: the church is now being restored to her pristine purity, being made fit for the bridegroom. Christ will only come back for a church which is pure and spotless, and she needs to make herself ready. Such an understanding is not new, of course. Usually it is referred to as "restorationism:" the church has lost a key aspect of the New Testament pattern, and that key is now being restored. Often such restorationism is linked to the return of Christ: when the church recovers the missing key, then Christ will come back for his bride. Restorationism was a common theme in nineteenth century revivalism and produced a host of new denominations which were convinced that God was busy restoring the New Testament church in their midst. If the rest of the church only got on board, then all would be sweetness and light. Sometimes the key was felt to be the recovery of the apostolic ministry (as with the Irvingites in Britain), sometimes an insistence on believer's baptism (as with Alexander Campbell's "Disciples of Christ"), while at other times the key was tied to a scheme of prophetic interpretation (as with the Seventh Day Adventists and the Mormons).

Such restorationism is inevitably divisive, and Wimber's version of it is already proving to be so. The conference showed a strong us-versus-them mentality: those who were on the "signs and wonders" bandwagon versus those who were just ordinary evangelicals (or even just run-of-the-mill charismatics). Wimber has used his interdenominational "renewal" conferences to extend his influence by reaching pastors and church leaders: he clearly gears his message to them. Pastors who had turned their backs on their own denominations or local fellowships testified that God had greatly blessed their ministry through their willingness to embrace Wimber's teachings. (So much for the "heinousness of division.") The fruit of such an emphasis is being felt in churches split in two by his zealous followers.

The Legitimacy of Concerns

Some will feel that these criticisms are unduly harsh, and one of

Wimber's supporters has privately questioned me about my motive for voicing them. Surely there must be something wrong with me spiritually to question aspects of Wimber's ministry. Nonsense, I reply. My motivation arises from a pastoral concern, for while many have been helped by John Wimber's ministry, many have been rightly upset by his actions, and others will, I fear, be disillusioned by the weaknesses in his theology. I am not willing to dismiss such people as rebellious; I will not shoot these wounded. His critics have legitimate concerns that need voicing, and his theology needs balancing.

Furthermore, as a church historian, I am aware that in the past the excesses of those who have sought to make much of the ministry of the Holy Spirit have produced severe negative reactions. This was the case with the Montanist movement in the second century. It was true of Luther, who reacted against the excesses of Thomas Muentzer and his followers in the early 1520s (to the extent that the Lutheran Reformation can be seen as an anti-charismatic movement). It was also the case with seventeenth century English Protestants, who were horrified with the "enthusiasts" who grew up during the period of the Puritan Commonwealth. In that case, the reaction led to a fear of any talk of the Holy Spirit and helped to pave the way for the rise of Unitarianism. My desire is to prevent a swing of the pendulum away from a legitimate concern with the Holy Spirit.

John Wimber would be the first to point out that no great work of God in history has been neat and tidy, nor has it fitted in easily with traditional forms and structures. God often comforts the afflicted while afflicting the comfortable. But surely such a realization should not be used to justify needless division and excess. And whatever one thinks about the wisdom of Wimber forming a new denomination, one can legitimately object to his doing so under the guise of a conference on "Signs and Wonders."

There is great potential for blessing from the positive features of Wimber's conferences. No doubt many Christians have benefited and will continue to benefit from his ministry. Balance, however, must be brought into certain areas. John Wimber makes it all too plain how much he hates the word "balance." He will be justly criticized if he continues to use his conferences to foster a new charismatic denomination. With its present direction and emphases, the movement is likely to produce negative reactions which in the long run will be detrimental to the working of the Holy Spirit in the church. The fault is not, as Wimber would suggest, with his listeners alone.

Part Three

THEOLOGICAL CONSIDERATIONS

What are the theological issues raised by John Wimber's teaching and the Vineyard movement? What does the Bible teach about signs and wonders, healing, the Holy Spirit, revival, divine providence? Six scholars give their responses.

Church Renewal for the 1980s?

John Vooys

The message John Wimber carries far and wide has an obvious basis in "kingdom theology" and shows the influence of George Eldon Ladd. Over against many a dispensationalist, Wimber sees no distinction between the kingdom of God and the kingdom of heaven—they are one and the same in scripture. The kingdom was ushered in by Jesus Christ's ministry on earth, although its full realization awaits his second coming. The kingdom is God's rule over everything, including Satan and his hosts.

Words and Works

Jesus demonstrated God's will on earth in his words *and* works. The two must not be separated. He not only taught his disciples truths, but he also trained and commissioned them to do what he did. Wimber emphasizes that Christ's modern disciples are to stand in that tradition and that commissioning. The Christian's ministry is to be to the whole person—salvation of the soul and healing of the body (spiritual, mental and physical). The Christian is to be involved in spiritual warfare because sin and Satan have brought death and general lack of wholeness into the world.

Christ has given his followers authority to teach what he taught and to do what he did. The Holy Spirit empowers the Christian, from conversion on, to minister through his indwelling presence and by means of spiritual gifts. Wimber loves to remind people that scripture teaches and church history shows that miraculous demonstrations of God's power did not cease with the death of the apostles or the completion of the New Testament. Their general *absence* in the modern church, rather than their presence, ought to be cause for surprise.

Clearly, Wimber seeks to bring about the equipping of the followers of Jesus. In his clinics he does little more than encourage and coach others into ministry so that they would speak to, pray for and lay hands on those in need. A brief paragraph from a brochure explaining one of Wimber's seminars sums up his goal in this regard:

> Our desire is to train as many believers as possible to have a ministry which includes the demonstration of the outworking of the power of the Holy Spirit in their lives. God has given us a vision to see the transformation of the Body of Christ from being an inactive audience to being a Spirit-filled army.

Putting Belief into Practice

Since the basic theology held by Wimber and the Vineyard is evangelical and biblical, and since Wimber's method of interpreting scripture is a sound one, there seems little ground for dispute here. The crux of concern seems to be in the outworking of the theology, the practice advocated by Wimber and his movement. As one pastor expressed it, "It is hard to refute Wimber's teaching from the Word. It is the application of it and the experiential aspect of it which is difficult!"

Many Christians hold to a theology and a statement of faith which is biblically sound. Many hold to the "priesthood of all believers," and rightly so. But what is to be made of every Christian actually putting into practice their beliefs? What of this "hands-on" ministry, ordinary followers of Christ waging spiritual warfare; praying boldly for healing of specific illnesses; using and responding to words of faith and knowledge; giving prophetic utterances; dealing with others (Christian and non-Christian) who are troubled by the evil one or his angels (the "demonized," to use Wimber's words)? Obviously such experiences outstrip the understanding of those of us for whom they are unusual.

That we have questions should not be surprising, for how are we to grasp the meaning of certain practices when we are unclear about the scriptural terms on which they are based? How do we understand the concepts of I Corinthians 12: messages of wisdom and knowledge; gifts of faith; gifts of healing; prophetic words? And what does one do with the idea of "demonization" (even of Christians)? Yet incidents related to Judas (Luke 22:3), Ananias and Sapphira (Acts 5:3), and Peter (Mark 8:3), cannot be dismissed out of hand.

If all the activity seems disruptive for some, the New Testament clearly shows that where the Holy Spirit is active, man's programs are often disrupted (as in the book of Acts) —and not always quietly. Even Peter was once disturbed mid-sermon (Acts 10:44-46)! Such truth caused someone to write, "When the Holy Spirit comes on men and women, there is new life. There is often disorder too—untidy edges. But give me this every time if otherwise I have to put up with cold, lifeless orthodoxy."

Final Assessment

How does one, finally, assess a teaching and a movement? It needs to be tested by the Word of God. We are instructed to "test the spirits to see whether they are from God" (I John 4:1-8). Even in this process one needs to be cautious, for two other texts are also helpful, though sobering. In Acts 5:38-39 Gamaliel advises the Sanhedrin in their judgment of the apostles' words and works, " . . . if their purpose or activity is of human origin, it will fail. But if it is from God, you will not be able to stop these men; you will only find yourselves fighting against God." In Matthew 12 the Pharisees credited Satan with work actually done by the Holy Spirit. Jesus called their action "blasphemy against the Spirit" (vs. 31).

Renewal movements have been sent by God to breathe new life

into his church. The Reformation revitalized the established church. One branch, the radical Reformation, sprouted Anabaptism and the Mennonite churches. In 1860 new life emerged again and led to the establishment of the Mennonite Brethren church. Could this new movement in the 1980s be intended to revitalize God's church again?

A "word" given to this writer and his wife by one of the participants at a Wimber seminar might also have relevance for the wider church: "You have been faithful, but the Lord wants you to let go and step out."

John Schmidt

I. THEOLOGICAL CONSIDERATIONS

The Spirit's Prominence

Looking at the teachings of the Vineyard, we note some important truths that evangelicals can affirm. The first is the prominence given to the person and work of the Holy Spirit. For many years the Holy Spirit was the neglected member of the Trinity, but in the past twenty years this has changed dramatically, especially through the emphasis of the charismatic movement. When encountering a new movement, we tend to react negatively, especially if it appears to overemphasize one aspect of truth, such as signs and wonders. An example of such a reaction concerns the Pentecostal movement. Until about twenty years ago, most evangelicals tended to regard Pentecostals as a cult because of their doctrine of baptism in the Spirit subsequent to conversion and speaking in tongues as *the* sign of such an experience.

Although we may not agree with all points on the baptism and filling of the Holy Spirit, we can affirm a movement that emphasizes the ministry of the Spirit in the believer's life. Jesus pro-

mised that the Helper who would take his place would empower
us for witness and service (John 14-16; Acts 1:8).

Gifts of the Spirit

A second truth we can affirm is that spiritual gifts are given for
service and should contribute to building the body of believers and
reaching unbelievers.

However, while the Vineyard claims to emphasize all the gifts of
the Spirit, an overview of its *Ministry Training Manual* shows that
the key gifts stressed are teaching, healing and exorcism—primarily
those dealing with signs and wonders. While we agree that healing
is a valid gift that can contribute to evangelism, it must be
recognized as only one of the many gifts the Spirit gives and should
not be elevated to a position of primary importance. Ben Patterson
raises a legitimate concern: "The ultimate goal of the Christian life
is fruit, not the gifts of the Spirit. It is not that the Signs and
Wonders people deny this; it is just that their emphasis on the gifts
of the Spirit impedes the ripening of the fruit."[1] When gifts are
overemphasized, it leads to an underemphasis on the ethical
demands of the gospel: what seems to be important is having
spiritual gifts rather than having Spirit fruit. The sign gifts can and
are being used to capture people's attention as a visible demonstration of the power of God. They can convince people of the presence
of God and can be used for evangelistic purposes. We can affirm
that but at the same time wish for a better balance. The verbal and
serving gifts are also given by the Holy Spirit and are as important
as those emphasized by the Vineyard movement.

Equipping Saints for Ministry

A third truth we can affirm is that every believer must be actively
involved in ministry and witness. The Vineyard teaches that all
believers are priests who minister with their gifts to the needs
within the body. Therefore, in their worship services, those giving
words of knowledge and prophecy and those praying for people in
need of healing are lay people who have been trained for this

ministry. This requires a large measure of faith. One Vineyard pastor admitted that it was rather disconcerting to see an 18-year-old praying for healing and God performing a miracle! The Vineyard practices the biblical truth of the priesthood of all believers, which has been made popular through Ray Stedman's emphasis on "body life." The apostle Paul makes clear in Ephesians 4:11-12 that the work of leadership is to equip the saints for ministry. This is an important biblical principle that needs continual emphasis in the church today. We rejoice in this biblical emphasis evident in Vineyard teaching.

Spiritual Conflict

A fourth truth, which comes from the Vineyard's kingdom theology, is the stress on the power of God to combat the forces of darkness, not just in Christ's day but in our day as well. That we are engaged in spiritual warfare is evident daily. The "power encounter" between the kingdom of God and the dominion of Satan is apparent all around us. The April 11, 1986 *Vancouver Province* carried the story of Jeffry Ewert, who murdered his girlfriend, stating at his trial that he was being driven by demonic powers. The powers of evil are real, but few Christians have become actively involved in exorcisms or dealing in personal ways with demonic forces. As the powers of darkness increase, we must heed Paul's admonition in Ephesians 6 to put on the full armor of God, to stand firm, to make use of the sword of the Spirit and prayer as mighty weapons against the forces of evil. This is especially so when we move out in evangelism, for then we are challenging the strongholds of the enemy and he will not let his people go without a tremendous battle. So we can affirm this strong emphasis on spiritual warfare.

II. PROBLEMATIC AREAS

The Kingdom and the Church

To understand the Vineyard movement we need to grasp the meaning of the kingdom as presented by John Wimber. Basing his understanding largely on the thinking of George Eldon Ladd, Wimber defines the kingdom (*basileia*) in the New Testament as the "exercise of kingly rule or reign rather than simply a geographic realm over which a king rules."[2] The *Vineyard Training Manual* says, "The purpose of the Vineyard is intertwined with our theology of the kingdom of God, which states that we are called to speak God's words, and do his works in order to re-establish his reign on earth."[3] Wimber explains that Christ's pattern of ministry was that of (1) proclamation: He preached repentance and the good news of the kingdom, and (2) demonstration: He cast out demons, healed the sick and raised the dead.[4] The church is to follow this two-fold pattern since the church has been given the keys of the kingdom (Matt. 16:19). "The keys," Wimber says, "are the narrow path to the kingdom of God."[5] Wimber follows Ladd's teaching that while the kingdom and the church must not be equated, the church witnesses to the kingdom, is an instrument of the kingdom and acts under the authority of the kingdom.[6]

That the kingdom was central to Jesus' ministry is clear from the gospel records. He began his ministry by preaching the kingdom of God (Mark 1:14-15), and that message continued to be a priority even after his resurrection (Acts 1:3). But the teaching of the kingdom is not nearly as evident in the ministry of the Twelve, as G. W. Peters points out.[7] It is Paul who went about proclaiming the kingdom (Acts 14:22; 19:8; 28:23,31) and who expounded the spiritual nature of the kingdom (Rom. 14:17). But the gospel of the kingdom was a "call to a radically new Lord . . . with a new citizenship and new demands. The emphasis is not on how easy but how costly it is to enter the kingdom."[8] Lewis Smedes writes that "Jesus himself told us that the call of the disciple is to a life of the cross, of self-denial, not to a life of reliance upon miracles to free us from the ailments and agonies that we are heir to on earth."[9]

This raises the significant question of whether the mandate Jesus gave his disciples to heal the sick, cleanse the lepers, cast out demons and even raise the dead (Matt. 10:1-5; Mark 6:7-13; Luke 9:1-6) was given to the church for all ages. Wimber would argue that it is so, because the church has the ongoing mandate to bring about the kingdom rule of God; therefore, we not only *can* but *must* do the works Jesus did. But, as Lewis Smedes points out, the mission Jesus gave the seventy was specific: it had the limited objective of preparing the way for Jesus' coming to those parts of the country. When conditions changed later on, the directions were different (Luke 22:35-36). Later still, after his resurrection, Jesus gave no mandate for a healing ministry. He told his disciples to go into all the world and make disciples, baptizing in his name and teaching them to obey all he had commanded (Matt. 28:19-20). They were given authority to forgive and retain sins (John 20:22-23), but Jesus gave no renewed commission to perform miraculous healings and exorcisms. Although there are indications of the apostles performing "signs and wonders," "Jesus' instructions to his disciples to prepare his way to the 'lost sheep of the house of Israel' are not the same as his instructions to his universal church. The disciples' mandate to heal the sick and raise the dead is not necessarily equivalent to the church's mandate."[10]

Wimber places primary emphasis on the kingdom. He can equate the mandate given to the disciples before the resurrection with that given after since, in his understanding, the church fulfills the kingdom mandate given in the gospels. This leads very naturally to his strong emphasis on the universal church and his tendency to downplay the local, visible church. The local church receives no mention in the "Theological and Philosophical Statements" of Vineyard churches. What is stressed is the demonstration and proclamation of the kingdom with visible manifestations of power; what is overlooked is the focus on the King and his desire to bring about his reign in the hearts and lives of believers. According to the Vineyard, only as miracles, signs and wonders bring glory to the King are the words of Jesus in reference to the coming and ministry of the Holy Spirit being fulfilled. G.W. Peters says it well: "The deepest miracle and the one most keenly and quickly sensed by the world is the miracle of the changed person. This is a miracle difficult to resist and impossible to disprove. The church should covet miracles of transformed lives more than anything else in this world."[11]

Suffering and Healing

The question of suffering has plagued mankind throughout history. Why does God allow suffering if he has the power to stop it? Why must some suffer so much, while others seemingly escape the pain and agony? Suffering is a mystery, one of the effects of the fall of man, something which continues to impact the human race.

God created man for wholeness of spirit, mind and body. However, J.I. Packer is right in insisting that there is serious danger in encouraging everyone who has an illness to always expect and only be satisfied with nothing less than physical healing. There is spiritual value, a maturing effect in "the discipline of suffering, going through pain with the Lord."[12] Sometimes sickness serves to chastise us or bring us to our senses and redirect our lives into a better course. In Packer's view, Wimber leaves no room for sanctification through suffering.[13]   In his article "When God Does Not Heal," J.H. Quiring wrestles with the issue of God not healing in answer to prayers uttered in genuine faith and all sincerity. He says concerning his daughter, who died of cancer at age 29: "She left us with the assurance that she was one of God's precious saints, sanctified in suffering."[14] To submit one's will to the will of God is the essence of prayer, which may produce far more profound healing of the spirit than of the body. "Suffering," writes Lewis Smedes, "is compatible with faithful Christian living, and . . . some suffering should be expected in anyone's pilgrimage."[15]

John Wimber follows the teaching of Father Francis McNutt, who suggests that too much emphasis has been placed on the "redemptive value of suffering, (so) that it has all but obscured the Good News of the gospel."[16] In another book on healing, McNutt argues that as Jesus was never sick, so believers should expect God to heal their illnesses.[17] While God can and does heal, Smedes argues, "We do not believe that Christian believers have a special entitlement to lasting health and instant healing."[18] Some of God's most noble saints are those who have suffered through long years of physical illness during which the work of the Spirit became very evident in their lives. Wimber himself carries nitroglycerine tablets for a coronary problem.[19]

Power Evangelism as the Focal Point

Wimber defines power evangelism as

> a presentation of the gospel that is rational but also transcends the rational. The explanation of the gospel comes with a demonstration of God's power through signs and wonders . . . . Power evangelism is that evangelism which is preceded and undergirded by supernatural demonstrations of God's presence.[20]

For many years our western world has been dominated by scientific rationalism, so that we have attempted to explain away much of the supernatural. As a result, a spiritual vacuum has been created alongside a lack of spiritual power in churches in North America. Martin Marty charges,

> We have become a nation of metaphysical shoplifters, spiritual window-shoppers, pious cafeteria-liners. In the end our religious being everywhere tends to be nowhere. Ministers become chaplains to ethnic groups, or persons who keep the doors open to preside at weddings. But they have a hard time representing the legitimate and biblical kinds of power.[21]

It is into such powerlessness that John Wimber and the Vineyard movement have come with their emphasis on power and on seeing the miraculous at work. A strong appeal is made to those in or near the church who are emotionally and spiritually starved and who long to experience more visible evidence of power in their lives.

However, to make signs and wonders the primary focus, based on texts like Hebrews 2:4 ("God also testified to it by signs, wonders and various miracles") is to misinterpret that text. Don Lewis reminds us that "the New Testament emphasis is on the proclamation of the gospel . . . . To become sidetracked on signs and wonders is to be entranced by sensationalism."[22] Jesus warned against this when he said, "A wicked and adulterous generation looks for a miraculous sign, but none will be given it except the sign of Jonah" (Matt. 16:4). The problem is that people are not moved unless they see something bigger and better each time. People may soon cease to wonder at the usual and seek for something new and different. The danger in wanting the spiritual heights is in not recognizing the marvels of God in nature or the daily wonders that may be very ordinary and are taken for granted. To make signs and wonders the key mark of a movement is exactly what some Pentecostals and some in the charismatic movement have done with Spirit baptism and tongues. This makes miracles the key factor and so tends to reverse the words of Jesus, "Blessed are those who have not seen and yet have believed" (John 20:29). The problem is in making power evangelism an end in itself, rather than a means to an end, namely conversion, which is the greatest miracle of all. Is there not the danger of becoming again that unbelieving generation which seeks for a sign?

Donald McGavran says, "I do not come from a church background that emphasizes healing. In fact, we have been a bit critical of it. Yet in my research I have discovered the winning of the lost has come in great numbers where men and women were healed in Christ's name. Amazing church growth has resulted."[23] Conversely, Colin Brown claims, " Very few people today seem to come to faith because of miracles. Most often it seems that people find that God in Christ meets their deepest needs."[24] He argues that nowhere in the New Testament are healings and exorcisms used as tools for evangelism. They are not designed to soften people to accept the message. Rather, he suggests, "Where the church has a ministry of caring and prayer for healing today, the focus should not be on the sensational. It should not be a kind of advertisement to pull people in . . . . It should be done in the name of Christ in order to meet the needs of the needy."[25]

In discussing "power evangelism," Wimber pits power against program, saying, "By its very nature and assumptions, programmatic evangelism tends to have as its goal decisions for Christ, not disciples."[26] His contention is that programmed evangelism lacks the demonstration of the power of the Spirit and so is not as effective as power evangelism. He says, "In programmatic evangelism there is an attitude that we do something and then God works. In power evangelism, God speaks and then we act." He suggests that programmed evangelism simply means going and sharing the message, whereas in power evangelism each evangelism experience is initiated by the Holy Spirit for a *specific* place, time, person or group . . . . In programmatic evangelism, the Christian says, "In obedience I go, Holy Spirit bless me." In power evangelism, the Christian says, "As the Holy Spirit tells me to go, I go."[27]

The assumption is that the only legitimate kind of evangelism is that done by signs and wonders. Such an assumption raises serious questions and is open to challenge, since throughout history many thousands have come to faith in Christ without ever having seen any kind of demonstration of power. The message of D.L. Moody, Billy Sunday, Billy Graham and a host of other evangelists has touched and transformed scores of lives without any visible demonstration of the kind of power events Wimber talks about.

Healings Occur Also in Folk Religion

Christianity has no monopoly on healing. There are many documented instances of healings attributed to numerous gods, spirits and healers. C.S. Lovett cites reports of healings performed by demons and adds,

Those of the religious science cults . . . are also able to obtain "miraculous" healings . . . . They have learned some of the laws which regulate the health of the human body and have discovered how to harness them for healing. Their work is valid, but they give no credit to the Lord Jesus, the Author of those laws.[28]

Colin Brown refers to testimonies of miracles performed by voodoo spirits in Latin America, south India and other places. He also notes that "from the early centuries onward the name of Jesus has been used in magic."[29] Jesus reminds us, "Many will say on that day, 'Lord, Lord, did we not prophesy in your name, and in your name drive out demons and perform many miracles?' Then I will tell them plainly, 'I never knew you. Away from me, you evildoers!'" (Matt. 7:22-23). We need a great deal of spiritual discernment in this matter, lest the Christian faith degenerate into a kind of pious magic.

Putting Experience above Scripture

While Wimber is conservative in his theology, some of his writings give the impression that experience is his starting point. He writes,

> Evangelicals believe that experience should not determine theology, that experience must always be subordinated to scripture . . . . Some truths in scripture cannot be understood until we have had certain experiences. I have found this to be the case with healing. Until I began to experience people being healed, I did not understand many of the scripture passages on healing.[30]

While there is some truth to this, to build a system of healing on this premise is highly problematic. To equate experience with facts is difficult, since facts are verifiable and experience is not. We must always place our experience under scripture and measure our experience by the revealed truths of God's Word, which are the facts. To begin with experience and then find verification in scripture is a shaky hermeneutic.

III. PRACTICAL QUESTIONS

While there are doubtless other problems and questions that could be raised in testing the new wine, we turn now to some practical considerations.

Is this a Genuine Movement of the Spirit of God?

Jesus reminds us that "a tree is known by its fruit," so we need to look at the fruit being born by this movement. Scores of people are being won to Christ. The rate of growth in Vineyard churches is phenomenal. Many people are being healed of physical, emotional and spiritual ailments. The gifts of the Spirit are functioning.

The Vineyard movement is impacting many people, both inside and outside the church. We cannot deny its existence as a genuine work of the Spirit, and so should not discredit it. We must not repeat what was done with Pentecostalism and think that by criticism we can wipe it out or that by silence we can ignore it and it will go away. We must recognize this as a new denomination which is attracting many people.

At the same time, we need to be aware of some of the extremes to which such a movement can go. Walter Unger says Wimber tends to quote Wesley, Whitefield, Edwards and Finney, all of whom describe signs and wonders similar to those found in the Vineyard movement. But he points out that the quotations are from their earlier writings rather than their later, more mature reflections. "Wesley and Edwards shifted considerably in their interpretation of what they at first called the 'wonderful bodily effects' attending their ministry."[31]

Most new movements of the Holy Spirit are embraced by eager followers, many of whom tend to push the ideas of the leaders to extremes. However, rather than write off the movement because of excesses, we should draw alongside to render guidance and counsel where it is needed and welcomed.

Why are Christians Being Attracted?

Why are Christians being attracted? While many reasons can be cited, one is the desire for something new or something more. Dissatisfaction with a lack of spiritual power, a feeling of unfulfillment in one's relationship to Christ and a hunger for a new and deeper experience with God are all factors. The Vineyard's emphasis on power, signs and wonders has a definite appeal to those who are searching for something more.

Also, many desire greater freedom in worship, something the Vineyard emphasizes strongly. A Vineyard service typically consists of 30 to 50 minutes of worship choruses. These are led by a musical team that encourages total participation by clapping and raising hands, standing or sitting, movement in dance and reaching out to one another in love. Many people are looking for love and acceptance and are finding it in the fellowship being offered in the Vineyard gatherings. There is a need in many churches for greater freedom in worship. This is not to say that all churches should adopt the Vineyard style of worship, but the emphasis on allowing the Spirit to minister in and through the worship experience is wholesome.

As well, some leave for the Vineyard because established churches are slow to change; this new movement, which downplays organized structures in favor of functional ministries, is attractive.

Another reason is that people will follow a leader who knows where he is going. John Wimber's background in business and marketing has provided a strong training ground for formulating and articulating clearly spelled out goals. That, along with his magnetic personality, enables him to gain a following.

Another reason is that many people's spiritual, social and physical needs have not been met in their churches. In some cases, there has been little clear teaching on the person and work of the Holy Spirit. Fundamentalism and dispensationalism have denied that the sign gifts are for this age, yet now these gifts are seen in operation. The danger is for the pendulum to swing to the other extreme. Some who have had a new experience through the Vineyard tend to start pushing their home church to adopt the same emphases. This causes a strong reaction, and the Vineyard advocate tends to leave in disillusionment or frustration. Throughout church history, doctrines have too often been formulated in opposition to a particular teaching rather than being based on proper study of the scripture. This happened when many evangelical churches developed their theology of the Holy Spirit in opposition to the teaching and practice of Pentecostalism. Rather than taking a defensive position concerning signs and wonders, churches need to search the scriptures honestly and seek to discuss openly what the Spirit is saying in this exciting era of church history.

Does God Always Heal?

Wimber believes that Christians should always expect healing, but that God may not always choose to heal. Al Camponi says that Wimber "teaches that healing can be a process, i.e., with every exchange of prayer there is a measure of healing." Such an emphasis comes from one of Wimber's teachers, Francis McNutt, who speaks of "soaking prayers," referring to the need to bring some illnesses to God over a long period of time.[32] Camponi goes on to say that Wimber

> believes that God always heals, maybe not according to our timing or wish, but he does heal. His explanation of failure extends the above argument. Not only may something be blocking the flow of healing from the sick person's vantage point, but the short-circuit may reside among those who are praying (sin, lack of faith, lack of knowledge as to how to pray, etc.).[33]

From the New Testament we note that not everyone was healed by Jesus. God is sovereign and may choose to heal some but not others. While Jesus never failed in healing, the apostles did. Trophimus was left behind by Paul at Melitus because of sickness (II Tim. 4:20). Paul had his thorn in the flesh (II Cor. 12:7). Timothy was told to use a little wine for the sake of his stomach and his frequent ailments (I Tim. 5:23). "Sometimes it is God's will that we have to live with our sickness and triumph in spite of it," writes Colin Brown.[34] Michael Green comments,

> God does not always choose to heal us physically, and perhaps it is as well that he does not. How people would rush to Christianity (and for all the wrong motives) if it carried with it automatic exemption from sickness! What a nonsense it would make of Christian virtues like longsuffering, patience and endurance if instant wholeness were available for all the Christian sick! What a wrong impression it would give of salvation if physical wholeness were perfectly realized on earth while spiritual wholeness were partly reserved for heaven! What a very curious thing it would be if God were to decree death for all his children while not allowing illness for any of them![35]

Just because God can perform miracles does not mean that he must or will. To insist that God will heal all Christians of every and any physical illness is to overlook the evidence of thousands of believers who have faithfully trusted God, some through many years of illness. What Colin Brown says is true: "The healing of the body is of much less importance than the healing of the soul. God's greatest gifts are the forgiveness of sins, peace with God, and eternal life."[36]

What about the Charge of "Sheepstealing"?

One Vineyard pastor's response to this charge was that "people are really not 'stolen'; they go where they are nourished, developed and can grow. When people come to a Vineyard church, they are asked to see their own pastor to get his blessing and release. . . . Most churches grow primarily by transfer." These are legitimate statements. Dr. MacGavran writes,

> During the past 50 years, most pastors in North America have leaned over backwards to avoid the charge of "sheepstealing." Partly as a result of this, about a hundred million Americans are nominal, marginal or slightly lapsed Christians. What is now demanded is that every church seek to be a better church—to have more biblical teaching, warmer fellowship, more Christian love, more concerns for social justice, and more effective evangelism of the lost. When a prospect says, "I belong to another church," he ought to be asked in as kindly a way as possible, "Are you a practicing Christian?" If the answers to these questions are not satisfactory, he (a sheep running wild on the range) ought to be found and folded, fed and transformed.[37]

One suburban pastor, who was charged with sheepstealing by the pastor of a downtown, nongrowing church, responded, "Splendid! You go on sleeping and we'll go on stealing."

While we are not advocating sheepstealing, we must acknowledge that most churches have grown mainly by transfers, not just from their own denomination but from other denominations as well. Is that then also sheepstealing, or is it sheepstealing only when our sheep go elsewhere? We must make a renewed effort to provide the kind of worship service that lifts up Jesus and the kind of loving fellowship that binds people together and meets their needs. Rather than merely pointing fingers at the Vineyards, let us take a closer look at why the wine in our own churches is not tasty enough to keep people in the fellowship. Perhaps our church or denomination is in dire need of renewal. If renewal comes through the Vineyard, let us rejoice in God's goodness and not cast stones because we fail to recognize what the Spirit is doing in this new denomination.

What about the Issue of Divisiveness?

We may deplore the need for another denomination, but we realize that most new denominations were the result of a schism. However, there is reason for concern when Ken Blue, pastor of the Vineyard Fellowship in North Delta, B.C., suggests that splitting churches is not bad but is one way to see church growth happen. Blue does not advocate splits but says, "genuine renewal movements are of God and they do split churches."[38] Such comments by leaders are picked up by followers who do not have the maturity or understanding to handle them, and so they add fuel to the fire rather than work toward understanding.

Part of the problem is the impression of elitism that comes through from some in the Vineyard who are overly zealous for their newfound experience of freedom and power. However, whether the Vineyard actually causes division in churches will depend not only on the attitudes of those who leave but also on the attitudes of those who stay. David Hubbard says that many pastors have expressed concern to him about the divisiveness of those who promote their spiritual gifts. When he asks pastors how they handle such people, the response is usually that the pastor tries to talk them out of their gifts or tells them to "shape up or ship out." The question then is, "Who is responsible for divisiveness, the enthusiastic charismatic or the pastor?" Hubbard writes,

> Change carries risks. But so does resistance to change. Change in an understanding of the Spirit's work may lead to excessive zeal that advocates "speaking in tongues" as the answer to all personal or social problems. But refusal to change may lead to deadly orthodoxy, smug spiritual complacency that assumes, "We know all truth and are totally satisfied with our level of spiritual maturity."[39]

How Should We Respond to this Movement?

We need to avoid the extremes of total rejection or wholesale acceptance of everything in the Vineyard. Both extremes are less than genuine wisdom. We should be open and honest in an ongoing evaluation of this movement to determine what is biblical and what is not. At the same time, we must continue to evaluate honestly our own churches to ensure that what we are doing is truly biblical and not merely tradition. We should affirm the positive aspects of this movement and help to strengthen the weak points. I pointed out to one Vineyard pastor his negative reflection on another denomination. His response was to invite further help in overcoming such weak areas. We need to come alongside this young movement and provide counsel and guidance—just as an older brother comes alongside a younger brother to help him grow and overcome hangups and problems. Those of us in denominations that have had the benefit of growth over many years need to share the wisdom gleaned from our experience rather than simply to sit back with a critical spirit. We can rejoice in the strong emphasis on renewal in worship; we can develop greater openness about healing; we can grow in our awareness of the powers of darkness; and we can learn from the strong emphasis on prayer. Let us not sit in judgment "lest we find ourselves fighting against God" (Acts 5:39) and lest, while the Vineyards blossom and bear fruit, we find him passing us by. We may not enjoy the initial taste of this new wine, but over time it may begin to provide a delightful spiritual flavor.

We Prayed for Healing . . . But She Died (What Does the Bible Teach about Physical Healing?)

Tim Geddert

We were sure God had promised healing; we thought that meant the cancer would not come back. But it did. We prayed for healing. We called the elders of the church to pray. We anointed with oil. We laid on hands. There were prayer vigils. There was fasting. We did everything that we could. We prayed every way we knew. Yet the dreaded disease brought about exactly the sort of physical and mental deterioration that the doctors had predicted. They suggested it would take between three and nine months . . . . It took five. Where was God? Where was his promise of healing? What about his promise that the prayer of faith would make the sick person well?

When cancer claims another victim, the survivors inevitably struggle with many questions: questions about the meaning of life and death, about the sovereignty of God and about the biblical texts which seem to promise healing if we pray in faith.

A Theology of Healing?

When our loved ones are dying, we cry out to God for spiritual resources to meet the crisis, and God gives them. But we also cry out to him for physical healing here on earth, and sometimes it is denied. Where does that leave the believer who reads the gospel accounts and gains the impression that everyone who came to Jesus for healing received it? Where are those "greater things" that Jesus said would be accomplished after he left? And what about James 5:14-18 and its promise that "the prayer offered in faith will make the sick person well"? Where does one find a biblically based "theology of healing" that matches with our experience, meets our needs and challenges our faith?

We will never find such a theology of healing as long as we insist on taking a single principle or model and trying to make it fit all the cases. Both the scriptures and the experiences of life are too variegated to be squeezed into one mold or model, no matter which one is selected. The model that says "God always gives healing if we pray with the right sort of faith" ignores about half the evidence of the scriptures. The model that says "Gifts of healing went out with the last of the apostles" ignores the irrefutable testimony of many modern believers. The model that says "God has chosen to limit himself in this age to what medical professionals can do" makes the same error and also misunderstands the nature of a doctor's work. The model that says "God is concerned with spiritual matters, not physical healing" is totally foreign to the principles that Jesus lived by. The model that says "God's ways are inscrutable; we cannot expect to understand" is a counsel of despair and short-circuits our responsibility to learn his ways. No single model is adequate. Each in its own way generates contorted biblical interpretations. Some of them also generate unnecessary and unfair loads of guilt ("You didn't pray in faith! Sin in your life blocked God's answer!"). Perhaps worst of all, they lead to theologies which rob the scriptures of their challenge and God of his sovereignty.

Because each model is inadequate on its own, we can hold to a single model only until it fails us. Then we find ourselves scrambling to find a better one. Unfortunately, we also castigate those with different models and call them unspiritual, unbiblical or unconcerned. I know whereof I speak. I have been a proponent of more than one model in my time. I have also been on the receiving end of advice from people in many camps. Simple answers are so attractive, but when they fail, then who will pick up the pieces?

I do not claim to have the definitive word on "healing," but I do urge that unless we find ways of holding several models in our theology at the same time, we will be unbiblical and we will be unprepared for the time when a cherished model fails. If we want to construct a well-rounded theology of healing, we would do well to begin at the critical text on prayer for healing, James 5:14-18. There are those who would urge that this text, above all others, warrants the conclusion that if we pray aright, healing will be granted. Does it really teach that?

The Prayer of Healing

James 5:14-18 teaches at least three things. It establishes a pattern: the sick call the elders to pray. It promises results: the sick will be healed. And it furnishes an example of how the model works: Elijah's prayers for a three and one-half year drought to begin and to end.

Have you ever wondered about the appropriateness of the example James uses? I have. Why Elijah? Moses and Elisha have more healings credited to them than he does. If it is important to cite Elijah, why mention the drought? Why not the time he raised the widow of Zarephath's son? It would seem more relevant to James' healing context. If it is important to mention a drought, why this one? The one in Jacob's time was twice as long. If the concern is simply to find a spectacular answer to prayer, why did James not look seven verses farther back? Surely fire from heaven is more amazing than rain! All in all, it seems James has selected a very strange example to prove his point; that is, unless perhaps we have misunderstood the real significance of the example and therefore also misread the passage about healing.

Remember the time Elijah was in despair because he thought he was the only faithful man of God left? Remember how God encouraged him by telling him that there were still seven thousand faithful men of Israel that he knew nothing about? What do you suppose they were doing during the three-year drought? I imagine they were praying for rain. I would have been. It would be the appropriate thing to do if the nation were perishing for lack of food and water. That is, it would be the appropriate thing if one did not know why the drought was happening and how long it would last. Seven thousand faithful believers pray for rain, and nothing happens. Were they lacking faith? Were they out of step with God? No, they were simply ignorant of God's purposes and his timing.

That is where Elijah was different. He knew the reason for the drought, and he knew its duration. He did not bother praying for rain until God's appointed time. When he knew the appointed time had come, he prayed, and, not surprisingly, it rained.

So why does James cite this example? Is it to tell us that whenever we pray fervently for a drought or for rain, we can expect it to happen? Hardly. Only one out of 7001 faithful Israelite prayers had that sort of success.

So what is the lesson about praying for healing? Is it to tell us that whenever we pray fervently for physical healing, we can expect to see the miracle? I think not. Does it not rather teach that if and when we have special insight into the purposes of God and the timing of his actions, then we can speak the authoritative "Stand up and walk!" and we can see it happen? Perhaps James 5:14-18 is focused far more on discerning God's doings than on priming the pump of faith.

I have read books on healing by those who are called "faith healers." Most of them say that there are particular times when they know with certainty that God intends to heal, and they can say with confidence, "Stand up and walk!" Maybe you do not believe any modern faith healer can *ever* speak with that authority. I will join you if you believe they cannot *always* do so. Modern faith healers aside, we can hardly deny that Jesus knew what would happen when he said that. So did Peter and John in Acts 3. If we know when and how God will heal, we can say "Stand up and walk!" with the same confidence, and it will happen.

A Balancing of Models

Is it not by now clear that the James 5 model does not cover all cases? Are we not much more often one of the seven thousand who do not know God's plans and whose prayers do not move God's hand? What then? If we insist that James 5 teaches that anyone can expect to see or experience a healing miracle if only his faith is what it should be, then we can expect to live under a load of guilt. If we read it as I am suggesting it should be read, then it is rather a challenge to be discerning people seeking to know God's doings and his timings, a challenge to pray with confidence for a miracle when he makes his intentions known, but a challenge to seek a more appropriate biblical model when he does not. But where do we turn for a supplementary model? We do not have far to look.

Which model would James have wanted to suppress at all costs if it had really been his concern to teach that physical healing in response to prayer was the norm, or even that knowing God's purposes and his timing was the norm? Obviously the example of Job. It simply does not fit the model. Job did not know why his disease was there. He did not know if or when his health would be restored. Moreover, the purposes of God in the case of Job could be fulfilled only because Job did not know. Ignorance of God's doings was as central to God's purpose for Job as knowledge of God's doings was for Elijah.

But James does not suppress the example of Job. On the contrary, he holds it up high right in the middle of James 5. Why? Because James never intended his readers to think that one model covers all cases. James knew that the Job model was also valid. It tells Christians something important about how God uses illness for his purposes and how and when he brings it to an end. And it gives believers another valid model for appropriate behavior in time of sickness. The Elijah model urges "effectual fervent prayer" when we understand what God is doing. The Job model urges "perseverance" when we do not (5:11). We cannot twist any single model and make it fit every case. A mighty miracle in response to prayer clearly brings honor to God. But so does a believer who perseveres without knowing why or how long he must suffer. The Job model puts its focus on "what the Lord *finally* brought about." That is why perseverance was so important. Job lived to experience not only physical healing but a doubling of his fortunes. In the end, God's character was vindicated, and Job experienced him to be "full of compassion and mercy" (5:11).

But what if neither the Elijah model nor the Job model fits? Not all live to experience God's merciful healing. Some die. We simply cannot in every case count on either God's miraculous healing (the Elijah model) or God's eventual doubling of our fortunes (the Job model). God's character is always vindicated in the end, but sometimes that end lies beyond the grave. Sometimes God expresses his compassion and his mercy by taking his child home, where sickness and pain are no more. When that happens, we realize that our "theology of healing" is incomplete without a third model, one which promises healing only in the life beyond.

James knew of this third model; he alludes to it in 1:12 and 4:14. So did the man who penned the seventy-third Psalm. He wrote of his struggle to find and accept this third model. It did not come easily. It troubled him when the wicked seemed to get a better deal in this life than the righteous—better health, greater wealth, fewer troubles. "When I tried to understand all this, it was oppressive to me till I entered the sanctuary of God; then I understood their final destiny" (73:16ff.). The psalmist learned that God is indeed good to the pure in heart (73:1) but that the measure of that goodness is not in health or wealth or happiness. "It is good to be near God." (73:28). The good news is that God is good when a prayer of faith raises the sick (the Elijah model), when we suffer, knowing neither why nor how long (the Job model) and even when suffering ushers us into glory (the psalmist model). "I am always with you," says the psalmist (73:23), "and being with you, I desire nothing on earth" (73:25).

James promises that "the prayer of a righteous man has great power in its effects" (5:16). It does indeed. Sometimes its effect is to change circumstances, and a sick person is dramatically healed (the Elijah model). Sometimes its effect is to change our characters, and we learn to persevere and trust the sovereignty of God (the Job model). Sometimes its effect is to change our priorities, and we rest in the assurance that "my flesh and my heart may fail, but God is the strength of my heart and my portion forever" (Ps. 73:26, the psalmist model).

We dare not build our theologies, our ministries or our lives on less than these three models. In some cases, the authoritative "Stand up and walk!" announces the miracle that God is bringing about. In some cases, long and patient suffering is crowned with restoration and blessing. In some cases, the flesh fails and mortality is swallowed up by life (II Cor. 5:4).

Many oversimplified and inadequate theologies of healing plague the Christian church. Almost all of them can be derived by selecting too few models. Pick any one or two of those suggested above and spin out the implications. You will see what I mean. When we set aside one valid biblical model in favor of another, we find ourselves twisting the biblical texts and our experiences out of shape to make them fit, or else we find ourselves burdened with guilt about the inadequacy of our faith.

What is needed is a theology that acknowledges all three models. Together they cover all cases. The only problem is that we do not always know in advance which model fits which case. And therein lies the challenge of the scriptures. The challenge is not one-dimensional but three, for we are called continually to discern God's ways, to persevere when we walk in the dark and to fix our eyes on things above, not on things on earth. In all this, God never fails us. If we draw nigh to him, he draws nigh to us, and therein we experience the good life that the writer of Psalm 73 discovered.

The Holy Spirit in
the Believers' Church

se

:J.B. Toews

The Holy Spirit has been prominent in the theological discussions of recent decades. The charismatic movement, with its strong emphasis on experience, on the "how" and "what" of the Holy Spirit's work, is affecting the church worldwide. "How" and "what," however, are insufficient as a basis for a biblical theology of the Holy Spirit. Nicodemus desired to understand Jesus' instruction that "unless one is born again, he cannot see the kingdom of God" (John 3:3, NKJV). He immediately asked, "How can a man be born when he is old?" Our Lord pointed out that the "how" is shrouded in mystery, "Do not marvel that I said to you 'You must be born again.' The wind blows where it wishes and you hear the sound of it, but cannot tell where it comes from and where it goes. So is everyone who is born of the Spirit" (3:7-8). Nicodemus somehow could not get beyond the "how." Again he repeated, "How can these things be?" (3:8). The second reply of Jesus pointed to the limitations of human understanding and implied that the mysteries of God are rooted in a relationship of faith, "As Moses lifted up the serpent in the wilderness, even so must the Son of Man be lifted up, that whosoever believeth in him should not perish but have eternal life" (3:14-15). At the center of the John 3 discourse is the relationship of humanity to the Son of God.

Therefore, a correct understanding of the Holy Spirit *cannot be drawn from the experiences of believers.* It must be based on understanding the Holy Spirit in relation to God and on understanding the Holy Spirit's purpose.

The Relationship between the Father, Son and Holy Spirit

No other part of scripture speaks more clearly of the relationship of God the Father, Jesus the Son and the Holy Spirit than John's writings. Let us focus on the concluding instructions of Jesus before he went to the cross as given in John 13-17. Chapter 13 contains the following statement: "Now the Son of Man is glorified and God is glorified in him" (13:31). Christ's approaching suffering and atoning death are referred to as glorifying the Father. (See also John 12:23-24,27-28.)

Chapter 14 provides further focus on Christ's relationship to the Father: "Do you not believe that I am in the Father and the Father in me? The words that I speak to you I do not speak on my own authority; but the Father who dwells in me does the work" (14:10). The promise of chapter 14, "whatever you ask in My name that will I do," is again rooted in the glorification of God the Father: "that the Father may be glorified in the Son" (14:10).

The instructions which follow in chapters 14 and 15 are an expansion of the relationship between the Father and the Son as outlined in chapter 13. The Holy Spirit is identified as the continued presence of the Father and the Son in the believer (14:16-20). Moreover, the continued relationship of the believer to God the Father and the Son is dependent on obedience to his commandments (14:21-24). The interdependence of the believer with the Son and the Father is further described in chapter 15, with the metaphor of the vine and the branches. The promise "ask what you desire and it shall be done for you" (15:7) is dependent on "if you abide in me and my words abide in you" (15:7) and is followed by "By this my Father will be glorified that ye bear much fruit; so you will be my disciples" (15:8).

It is within this setting that chapter 16 presents the assignment of the Holy Spirit:

He will convict the world of sin and of righteousness and of judgement . . . . He will guide you into all truth; for he will not speak on his own authority, but whatsoever he hears, he will speak . . . . He will glorify me for he will take of what is mine and declare it to you. All things that the Father has are mine. Therefore I said that he will take of mine and declare it to you (16:8,13-14).

The interrelationship of the Godhead appears very clearly in John 13-16. The center of the Godhead is the Father God. The Son is the manifestation of the Father (14:12-15). The Holy Spirit shall come from the Father and shall glorify the Son (16:12-15).

The Assignment of the Believers' Church

John 17 must be viewed in the context of chapters 13-16. John 17:1 restates the purpose of Christ's assignment: "Glorify your Son, that your Son also may glorify you." Verse 18 then passes on that assignment to the church: "As you sent me into the world, I also sent them into the world." The four-fold "I have" in verses 4-8, which defined Christ's assignment in the world, thus also defines the assignment which has now been committed to those who will believe in Jesus:

1. *"I have glorified you on the earth"* (17:4). As we have seen in chapters 13-16, the center of Christ's assignment was to glorify the Father in complete surrender of his own independence. John 5:31; 7:17,28,42,54; 10:18 and 12:49 underline the same truth. The first sin in E~en was man's rebellion against God. The contrast in Christ is summarized ir his words in John 3:34: "My meat is to do the will of him that sent me and to finish his work."

2. *"I have finished the work which you have given me to do"* (17:4) announces the completion of Christ's commitment stated in John 3:34. This declaration is repeated in Christ's cry from the cross: "It is finished" (John 19:30). In becoming the sacrifice for our sins, Christ glorified the Father.

3. *"I have manifested your name to the men whom you have given me out of the world"* (17:6). The identity of Christ with God the Father is expressed clearly in John 14:7: "If you had known me you would

have known my Father also." This identity is also central for "those who will believe in me," as expressed in the prayer of 17:18: "that they all may be one as you Father are in me and I in you; that they also may be one in us." (See also II Corinthians 6:16, Ephesians 3:16-17, Colossians 1:27 and the prophetic passages, Leviticus 26:12, Jeremiah 32:38 and Ezekiel 37:27.)

4. *"I have given to them the words which you have given me" (17:8)* extends the assignment to proclamation.

The commission of Christ, "As you sent them into the world, I have also sent them into the world," leaves no room to question the purpose or calling of believers in the world. The burden of the Lord's "High Priestly Prayer" in John 17 is for the believing community to express the character of God. Here is the primary calling of the church in the world.

The Great Commission of the Church

Is it possible that the emphasis on world evangelism and missions of the twentieth century has clouded the true New Testament purpose of the church in the world? Has the "lostness" of human beings become central in our understanding, as we see the gospel primarily as a means to escape the consequences of sin? Have we lost the true meaning of Christ's Great Commission to the church in Matthew 28:18-20?

In the Great Commission, "Go therefore" is prefaced with "All power has been given unto me in heaven and on earth." The emphasis on the pre-eminence of God the Father is evident.

"Make disciples"—the verb is imperative—places the emphasis not on salvation but rather on a recognition of Jesus as Lord and submission to him. Regarding discipleship, Jesus says, "If any one comes to me and does not hate his father and mother, wife and children . . . and his own life . . . . and whosoever does not bear his cross and come after me . . . . (and) does not forsake all that he has *cannot be my disciple"* (Luke 14:25-26,33).

"Baptizing them" is also part of the commission. In the theology of Paul, this is an identification with Christ in death and a commitment to walk in newness of life (Romans 6:2-13).

"Teaching them to observe *all things* that I have commanded you" is also part of the Great Commission and is directly related to the purpose of the redeemed community.

The Purpose of the Holy Spirit

Chapters 13-17 of the Gospel of John point to the *theo*-centricity (God-centeredness) of the Holy Spirit's purpose in the world. The tendency in recent decades to place a major emphasis on experiences of the Spirit—gifts, miracles and wonders, speaking in tongues and the healing of the sick—poses a danger. The gifts of the Spirit (I Cor. 12:1-11) are identified with the recognition of the Lordship of Christ (12:3). Paul, through the Holy Spirit, places I Corinthians 13 at the center of the discussion of these gifts. This love chapter calls for self-denial and giving God the pre-eminence. The promise of Christ to his disciples, "Whatever you ask in my name, that will I do, *that the Father may be glorified in the Son*" (John 14:12-13), remains the only premise on which we can ask for a manifestation of the Holy Spirit in the form of signs and wonders.

In the progressive revelation of God, the fact that the emphasis on signs and wonders is absent in the apostolic writings after Acts cannot be ignored. The central concern of the early church was that the life of the believers might glorify God, "We are children of God . . . heirs of God and joint heirs with Christ, if we indeed suffer with him, that we may also be glorified together" (Romans 8:17). The light given to us to know God serves to the glory of God in Christ Jesus (II Cor. 4:6). Paul's prayer for the church is that it "be filled with the fruit of righteousness . . . to the glory and praise of God" (Phil. 1:11). Paul's admonition to the church is "Whether you eat or drink or whatever you do, do all to the glory of God" (I Cor. 10:31). The calling of the church is "that God in all things may be glorified through Jesus Christ" (I Peter 4:11). After reviewing our human perplexities, sufferings and adversities—which may include illness for which we do not find healing—Paul concludes, "For all things are for your sakes, that grace, having spread through the many, may cause thanksgiving to abound to the glory of God" (II Cor. 4:15).

It is in this context that the purpose of the Holy Spirit in the church must be understood. "He will glorify Me" (John 16:14) remains the test of genuineness.

A Spirit-filled Life

The biblical teaching considered above is a call to examine trends in evangelical circles in the western world. The strong emphases on evangelism, missions and salvation theology have resulted in underemphases on Christology and the central purpose of the Holy Spirit. Salvation is perceived as a benefit separate from the demand of biblical discipleship. Evidence of the indwelling of the Holy Spirit is sought in power manifestations such as tongues, miracles, signs and wonders. The charismatic phenomenon makes a strong appeal to a bewildered culture of pragmatic individualism. II Thessalonians 2 and II Peter 2 warn against the deception of false teachings that are made attractive by supernatural phenomena. These warnings need to be heeded. In the last few months, some of the most widely known religious ministries have become a mockery to the world—their claims of spiritual power have proven to be deceptions because of inconsistencies between message and life. In view of this, the emphasis on supernatural experiences must be examined anew. The evidence of the Holy Spirit is a character that glorifies God. A godly person lives in tension with the world. Salvation is not a mere benefit (assurance of eternal life) but a commitment to self-denial and a walk of holiness. The claim of a Spirit-filled life must be tested by the fruit of the Spirit (Gal. 5:22-26), not by subjective experiences and benefits. The miracle of the Christian faith is a life of purity and holiness lived by one who has died to self, a life that reflects the image of the marvellous Christ who knows only one passion: that God be glorified.

The Miraculous in Ministry

Art Glasser

The charismatic renewal movement poses a massive challenge to evangelical Christianity. Without structured organization or unified leadership, it has penetrated all six continents, left no Protestant denomination unmoved, and leaped the high walls of Catholicism and Orthodoxy. All elements of traditional Christianity have been influenced. Never has there been such a challenge to their theologies, worship patterns and churchly practices. Although the movement is multiform, its uniformities are significant. Its focus is on experienced fellowship with Christ and other Christians (I John 1:3). Its appeal is in the warmth and support of caring groups, made possible through the conviction that all Christians may minister to one another because they have spiritual gifts. The Roman Catholic theologian Francis Sullivan has even stated:

> Not a few prominent theologians are convinced that the future of Christianity in secular, unchristian, if not anti-Christian society, is going to depend on the vitality of such spontaneous groups and communities of committed Christians as are form- ing through the charismatic renewal. What some are inclined to fear as the beginning of a sect may well turn out to be a pillar of strength for the church of the future.[1]

That the basic postulates of this movement are biblically sound needs little defense. It has unabashedly brought onto center-stage the realities of New Testament *koinonia* (fellowship), the activity of the Holy Spirit and the experience of direct contact with the living God through the redemptive death and victorious resurrection of Jesus Christ. Its sheer numbers of radically transformed people making common confession of Jesus Christ as Lord and Savior are most impressive. No longer can the conduct of charismatics be dismissed as evidence of psychological imbalance, or worse.

Even so, within this extensive movement one encounters much that gives reason for pause. Extravagant claims abound. There is a preoccupation with the miraculous. Social responsibility is downplayed; political quietism is tolerated. Psychological manipulation is occasionally uncovered, and the recourse to magical formulas is not uncommon. What is perhaps most offensive is the tendency to preach a "prosperity gospel" that guarantees material blessing for the believer. Despite all this, evangelicals need to take fullest measure of the movement, remembering that it is always best to be "swift to hear" but "slow to speak" (James 1:19).

In my experience as a missionary in Asia, I was often confronted with signs and wonders, tongues and exorcism, but these were largely found in Buddhism and Hinduism. Hence, in any discussion of the miraculous, the central issue must be: how to discern the activity of God's Holy Spirit from that which comes from elsewhere. A second issue is the nature of the gospel of Jesus Christ: what is its ultimate objective in the lives of those who believe—is it to be charismatic or ethical?

How are we to understand biblically the role of the miraculous in Christian ministry and use this as a basis for evaluating the charismatic renewal movement? Although little precise agreement exists within the movement itself on such matters as speaking in tongues, words of knowledge, prophecy, healing and exorcism, it is the prominence given to these allegedly "miraculous" phenomena that gives concern to those seeking biblical balance. Why this concern? Because on every hand we hear that all these phenomena are from God. Furthermore, because they allegedly demonstrate that at long last the Christian movement worldwide is becoming biblically holistic.

A second concern arises from the apostle Paul's fear "that the cross of Christ be emptied of its power" (I Cor. 1:18). As a result, he made the gospel central to his ministry. The cross to him uniquely represented "the power and the wisdom of God" (I Cor. 1:24). In his day Christians sought to avoid the offense, the rejection and the shame that came because of their public identification with the cross of Christ (Gal. 5:11; 6:12). Hence, Paul's desire was to glory in nothing "except in the cross of our Lord Jesus Christ" (Gal. 6:14). Evangelicals must guard this centrality and not allow it to be supplanted by any less important theme. The present great interest in the miraculous can easily divert attention from the cross of Christ.

Biblical Reflections

When we consider the biblical data, we discover that a distinct shift in emphasis exists between the gospels and Acts and the remainder of the New Testament. While the gospels present Jesus as a miracle worker and the Acts portray certain key persons in the early church as performing miracles, Paul in his epistles seems reluctant to recall his own involvement in this activity and even downgrades its importance. Rather, he, James and the apostle John, stress ethical concerns and call attention to the need for discernment, for testing the spirits. Their approach to spiritual realities is greatly different from current charismatic emphases.

Admittedly, the synoptic gospels attribute Jesus' fame to his miracles (e.g., Mark 1:28). Even so, the purpose of the miracles was revelation, in the sense that they identified him as the Messiah portrayed in Isaiah (Is. 35:5-6; 61:1; cf. John 20:30,31). The blind saw, the lame walked, the dumb heard and the mute spoke (Matt. 11:4-6; Mark 7:37). When he rebuked demons or caused the raging sea to be still, he was vividly demonstrating God's hostility to all that corrupts or disturbs his good creation. "The miracles of Jesus are eschatalogical signs: they announce the coming of the Messiah, restore the original purity of creation and deny the authority of Satan over that creation."[2]

Furthermore, it is significant that once the disciples confess Jesus' messiahship, the focus shifts to his coming suffering: his rejection by the Jews, his crucifixion by the Romans and his resurrection by the power of God (Matt. 16:13-23). Miracles diminish in frequency. The pattern likewise characterizes the disciples. Initially, they are commanded to "heal the sick, raise the dead, cleanse lepers (and) cast out demons" (Matt. 10:8), but they too increasingly enter into Jesus' experience of rejection and suffering. The Great Commission, apart from the spurious ending of Mark (16:9-20), contains no suggestion that the miraculous will be normative in the performance of their worldwide mission.

Even so, the book of Acts reveals continuity with the earlier picture of Jesus in the gospels. His disciples are miracle workers. "Signs and wonders" and miracles of healing appear frequently (2:22,43; 4:30; 5:12; 6:8; 14:3; 15:12; 19:11,12; 28:8,9) and serve as revelatory signs of the messianic movement of the resurrected Christ. They provide evidence of its ongoing validity as it emerges from the Jewish context. A universal faith has legitimately evolved from God's dealings with a particular people. As a result, the book of Acts is replete with evidence of the power of God. Judgment falls on hypocrites (5:1-11). Apostles are miraculously delivered from prison (5:17-23; 12:1-11), from shipwreck (27:39-44) and from a poisonous serpent (28:3-6). All the while, the Holy Spirit empowers their preaching, converts Jews and gentiles alike, supernaturally directs their mission and in other ways demonstrates his presence in their midst.

However, when we enter the world of the epistles, can we detect a shift in emphasis? True, Paul refers to "signs and wonders" in a summary of his years of ministry in the northeastern Mediterranean (Rom. 15:19), and he is looking forward to an extension of his pioneering ministry into the western Mediterranean, presumably expecting further "signs and wonders" to accompany his witness of the gospel (Rom. 15:23,24). He defends his apostolic authority to the Corinthians by claiming to have performed "the signs of a true apostle . . . with signs and wonders and mighty works" (II Cor. 12:12). In similar fashion, Paul reminds the Galatians that the miracles that accompanied their first hearing of the gospel were evidence of the Spirit's confirming work (Gal. 3:5).

However, when Paul deals with spiritual gifts in I Corinthians 12, we find "gifts of healing" (12:9) and "working of miracles" (12:10) on a lower level of importance when contrasted with the apostolic, prophetic and pastoral gifts, in which the ministry of the Word is paramount (12:27-31). He goes to great lengths to warn of the possible abuse of the gift of "tongues" (I Cor. 14). From all this one concludes that the mere performance of miracles and healings is distinguished from the "signs and wonders" that were the marks of a true apostle (II Cor. 12:12).

What should we conclude from this data? Surely, in Pauline churches miraculous deeds and physical healings took place. Furthermore, ordinary Christians performed them. One gains the impression, however, that these happenings did not express the distinctly revelatory character of the messianic community, such as we find in the Acts. After all, in the Acts Luke was seeking to establish the validity of this new messianic community and to identify the sequence of events that separated it from the Jewish synagogue.

Furthermore, Paul's references to sickness, physical infirmity and material want among the members of his missionary team must be placed alongside his unqualified gratitude to God for forgiving their sins and bestowing new life in Christ. Apparently he was convinced that God had not promised healing but had guaranteed forgiveness. Not all Christians are strong, healthy and materially prosperous, but all the truly regenerate have been saved.

What impresses one particularly is Paul's approach to the critical events in Jesus' earthly life. The greatest miracle—the resurrection—is not regarded as miraculous in the classical sense (i.e., as a violation of the laws of nature, I Cor. 15:3,4,20-23). Paul's concern is to show that the continuing life of the people of God beyond physical death is based on the reality of their "in-Christness." They are united with him in death, burial and resurrection. The resurrection of Christ guarantees their resurrection after death. Interestingly, Paul makes no reference at all to the miraculous in Jesus' earthly ministry.

Furthermore, Paul does not present himself as one who performed the works attributed to him in the Acts: healing the sick or raising the dead. Admittedly, he has had ecstatic experiences (II Cor. 12:1-4), but he prefers to dwell on his weakness and suffering (II Cor. 11:22-12:21). He does not tell Timothy that he expects to be delivered from prison (II Tim. 4:9-18). What then is he trying to say to us in his epistles? Is he encouraging us not to seek for charismatic experiences but to devote ourselves to developing personal and corporate character? Not quite, for Christians must always be on tiptoe expectation that their unpredictable God is able on occasion to do the unexpected (Eph. 3:20). Even so, justice, mercy, faith—the three obligations of the old covenant (Micah 6:8)—are expanded to include "peace and joy in the Holy Spirit" (Rom. 14:17). These are central signs of the kingdom of God. Indeed, when Paul speaks of the kingdom, he is quick to assert that it "does not consist in talk, but in power" (I Cor. 4:20). Was he referring to "signs and wonders"? This is an outside possibility, but I cannot get away from our Lord's beatitude on those who deny themselves the selfish luxury of remaining neutral in the face of the moral and social issues of the day (Matt. 5:10). To suffer for righteousness' sake is a far more compelling demonstration of the presence of the kingdom than any healing meeting— even though we readily grant that on occasion God heals the sick.

Paul's concern is for the church's social responsibility (e.g., "remember the poor," Gal. 6:10), as well as for its evangelistic outreach (e.g., "become all things to all men . . . (to) save some," I Cor. 9:22). Hence, if Paul were here today, I feel he would challenge our preoccupation with the charismatic and call us to enlarge our understanding of the church's total ministry. Best says,

> It is not that miracles are either invalid or superfluous, but that they do not meet the primary needs of Paul's congregations. The great charismatic and miracle-working individual— Jesus—has come and gone, and it is now time to get about the business of institution-building. And here it is not miracles, but the ability to relate to one another creatively and lovingly while maintaining a distinctive identity over against the surrounding culture, which is decisive.[3]

It is rather significant that Paul's final letter (II Timothy) contains an appeal to hold fast the deposit of truth contained in the Old Testament scriptures and the climax of God's revelation in the person and work of Jesus Christ (II Tim. 1:13,14; 2:10,11; 3:15-17). No mention is made of the miraculous; the stress is rather on "suffering for the gospel" (1:8; 2:3,11), "rightly handling the Word of truth" (2:15) and "doing the work of an evangelist" (4:5). Since

Paul makes no mention of signs and wonders, this raises the question, are they normative to the mission of the church?

All this is in sharpest contrast to the growing preoccupation with "power evangelism" in large segments of the charismatic movement. As stated above, Paul's constant fear was "that the cross of Christ be emptied of its power" (I Cor. 1:18). As far as he was concerned, the kindness of God displayed in the cross is what leads people to repentance (Rom. 2:4). The power inherent in the gospel must not be downgraded (Rom. 1:16). Hence, along with Jesus, he condemned the popular desire for signs, since to demand them indicated nothing less than the deliberate refusal to respond to the truth already given. Does this mean that Jesus' promise of "greater works" must not be understood literally in the physical sense? Should the focus be on the results the apostles would achieve through the proclamation of "Christ crucified," a stumbling block to Jews who "demand signs" and folly to Greeks who "seek wisdom," but to those who are called, both Jews and Greeks, Christ the power of God and the wisdom of God (I Cor. 1:22-25)?

It is significant that the sole instruction in the epistles on praying for the sick (James 5:14-16) is silent regarding the exercise of any gift of healing. Its overarching objective is that spiritual renewal might also come to the afflicted through their confession of sin. There is also no mention of special healing meetings or of healing activities to soften up people so they will believe the gospel. Does this mean that in the early church healing largely took place within the caring Christian community and was not related to anything approximating any so-called "power evangelism"?

The Cruciality of Discernment

Up to this point, we have not directly referred to the apostle's orders that the church's total deposit of truth be guarded against "deceitful spirits" and "doctrines of demons" (I Tim. 4:1; II Tim. 1:14) or that the spirits be tested "to see whether they are of God" (I John 4:1). Many who desire to be most open to the positive dimensions of the charismatic movement are often disturbed by the absence of heeding this counsel in the churches it has influenced. This neglect has greatly detracted from their credibility and has brought into question the extravagance of their claims.

Scripture clearly indicates that the Christian community should be able to distinguish truth from error by the simple means of "examining the Scriptures daily to see if these things (are) so" (Acts 17:11). This becomes possible only when Christians "devote themselves to the apostles' teaching and fellowship, to the breaking of bread and the prayers" (Acts 2:42). Then they increasingly gain the ability to discern truth, reject error and through collective discussion come to a sense of the will of God, the Holy Spirit being their guide.

But discernment extends beyond the realm of ideas. Christ warned of false prophets who come in sheep's clothing (Matt. 7:15), who perform all manner of "signs and wonders," and whose counsel often appears most wise and judicious. The community of faith must learn how to test them and by rejecting their witness, preserve its integrity. Indeed the scriptural mandate to test them is pressed home upon the people of God (I Cor. 12:3; I Thess. 5:19-22; Rev. 2:2). In the older covenant, Israel was to investigate thoroughly the credentials of anyone who posed as a prophet of God (Deut. 13:14; 18:22).

Often a false spirit betrays his dominance of a human being by what he does not say. For instance, according to I Corinthians 12:3, this spirit may say many plausible things, but if he continually, almost studiously, avoids making any reference to the lordship of Christ, one should consider asking him directly whether he acknowledges that Jesus Christ has "come in the flesh." Attention is thereby focused on the incarnation. According to I John 4:2-3a, any denial of this great truth would be evidence of "the spirit of antichrist" and not of the Holy Spirit. Fortunately, many of God's choice servants down through the years have experienced the wisdom of such specific probing. All too often, to their surprise and horror, they have uncovered the voice of the enemy of our Lord Jesus Christ and have resisted his presence and speech in the name of the risen Christ. The very fact that "many false prophets have gone out into the world" (I John 4:1) is a call to both vigilance and obedience to the mandate to "try the spirits." The risen Christ commended the church in Ephesus for having "tested those who claim to be apostles but are not, and . . . found them to be false" (Rev. 2:2).

In addition, attention should be called to the statement that "every spirit which does not confess Jesus is not of God" (I John 4:3). It is significant that a definite article (*tou*) preceded the name of our Lord. Does the apostle John want us to realize that an evil spirit may confess to *a* "Jesus" of its own creation and not to "*the* Jesus,*"* who is specifically the incarnate Christ—the One whom John had "seen and heard" (I John 1:3)? Most assuredly! The mere use of the name "Jesus" is insufficient. Such passages reflect the concern of the early church to protect the community of faith from carelessly following any teacher merely because he or she spoke much of Jesus. The test was to make sure the witness was to the One who "was in the beginning with God" and who "became flesh and dwelt among us" (John 1:2,14).

Anyone who has been exposed to the endless attempts to reconceptualize Jesus of Nazareth to suit the mood of the moment can bear witness to this activity of "the spirit of antichrist." How futile have been the attempts to categorize Jesus according to one or another of the diverse groups in the Judaism of his day or according to the religious sentimentalism of our day. So then, the apostle keeps saying to the church down through the centuries, "Stop believing every spirit." This has no reference to those who were professed pagans but to people who claimed to be Christians, who claimed to possess the Holy Spirit and who claimed therefore that they had profound spiritual insight into truth (2:18-28). As George S. Barrett states, "They spoke, as it seemed, with a Christian tongue, but nonetheless they were deadly opponents of Christianity and Christ . . . hence the urgency" of John's warning.[4]

In this connection, E.M. Blaiklock wisely counsels,

> We are not to be eager to impute error, to find fault and heresy where none is intended. We are not to apply tests and canons of our own invention, eager to demonstrate that all the rest are wrong, and we alone are right. Too often has orthodoxy shown that spirit, and antagonized where it might have reconciled and spoiled all testimony to truth by a lamentable lack of love.[5]

This counsel is well taken. It is significant that the remainder of I John 4 contains a most comprehensive development of love—its source in God and its perfection in the lives of Christians (4:7-5:2).

However, I am pressed to repeat: many religions have their practitioners who exorcise demons, speak in tongues, work signs and wonders, and heal the sick. Paul said that the antichrist would have these capabilities (II Thess. 2:9). And John stressed that "many antichrists have come" already into the world and seek to seduce the elect of God (I John 2:18-27). This being so, it is crucial that the church stress the need for discernment: how to identify the activity of God and how to distinguish it from that which is devoid of his impulse or even deliberately contrary to his will. Since scripture clearly spells out the fruit of his Spirit (Gal. 5:22,23) and thereby provides us with unambiguous evidence of his presence, there is no excuse for Christians not being willing to "test the spirits to see whether they are of God."

The greatest shame that came to the evangelical movement worldwide during 1987 and 1988 was the exposure of immorality and self-indulgence on the part of charismatic TV preachers whose programs continually boasted of God working "signs and wonders" in their midst. These individuals were never examined by their church leaders as to their spiritual integrity. Because they were successful in terms of attracting incredible numbers of people and raising unbelievable sums of money, their ministry was widely endorsed by charismatics. One wonders what might have happened had the biblical injunction to "test the spirits" been pressed upon them during the course of their ministry. Could this disaster have been averted?

Pastoral-ethical problems are invariably created when the claims of the more flamboyant charismatics are not fulfilled. One then becomes greatly troubled over the rationalizations, the juggling of facts, the silences, the violations of ethical integrity that are used to bolster the honor of God when public affirmations are not realized, when prophetic utterances are not confirmed and when those whose expectations have not been realized are not cared for. This focus on the charismatic tends to impede movement toward the ultimate objective of the Christian, which is not charismatic but ethical. Those most preoccupied with physical and demonic realities appear least interested in responding to the ethical and social issues of our day: justice for the poor and minority peoples, opposition to all forms of racism, sexism and exploitation, and the promotion of disarmament and world peace.

Conclusion

So then, we conclude with the observation that the church is not to judge its doctrines by the evidence of the miraculous, but rather it is to judge the seemingly miraculous by scripture. When tongues or words of knowledge or healings or even striking evidence of church growth are present, this does not automatically mean that they are all of God. Further proof is needed. Anything that happens but which on examination contradicts the teaching of Christ and his apostles is not of God. It is for this reason that we cannot but be concerned when in the euphoria over ''what is happening in our church!'' one detects the strange absence of any testing of the spirits. May our loyalty to Jesus Christ and to truth make us vigilant when messages are proclaimed (I John 4:2,3) and when people are attracted (I John 4:5,6)—all this with the sweeping boast that God is in the midst of his people. The spirits must be tested because ''many false prophets have gone out into the world.''

Paul G. Hiebert

In recent years there has been a renewed interest in miraculous experiences in the church. The Pentecostals emphasize tongues and prophecies as proofs of God's presence among his people. The charismatics look for such evidences in ecstatic experiences. Now, in many churches, on television and in conferences, the focus has shifted to healing, exorcisms and words of knowledge. One example is John Wimber and the Vineyard movement.

What should our response be to this renewed interest in miracles? As Norman Cohn points out, the issues involved are not new.[1] Periodically in the life of the church there have been leaders calling for miraculous demonstrations of God's power as signs of his presence among his people. St. Gregory, living in the sixth century, describes in detail a preacher from Bourges who healed the sick who were brought to him and gathered a large following. A century and a half later, St. Boniface described another itinerant preacher, Aldebert, who claimed to perform miraculous cures and attracted large audiences. Others followed. Many claimed that the kingdom of God had come in its fullness for those who believe. The results of their ministries were mixed: sometimes the church experienced renewal, but often it was led astray and left in disarray and divided. The same is true of revival movements in which the focus on present problems and miraculous solutions became central.

Today we again hear many prophets claiming new revelations and special relationships with God. We need to understand the times, and we need to heed John's exhortation and test their messages against scripture as it is interpreted within the community of believers.

I. UNDERSTANDING THE TIMES: THE RISE OF THE MODERN WORLDVIEW

The renewed interest in miracles in the Western church today is due in large measure to changes taking place in the foundations of our ways of thinking—in our "worldviews." Underlying every culture are basic assumptions about the nature of things. These are simply taken for granted. If someone questions them, he is seen not as wrong, but as foolish. For example, in the West if we were to argue that freedom is not inherently good for a society, people would not take us seriously. These assumptions are the lenses through which we view the world.

Currently the Western world is undergoing a radical change in its worldview. The old foundations that provided the basis for Western thought for some two or more centuries are crumbling, and no one set of new foundations has replaced them. In such times of uncertainty and fear, prophets often emerge, proclaiming new worldviews which, they promise, will guide people to a better life. This is true today, both in science and religion. It is within this flux that we must understand the movements of our day.

The modern worldview that has served the West for the past two centuries was deeply influenced by both the Reformation and the Renaissance. During the Middle Ages, the church regarded this world as essentially evil, a place in which Christians suffered on their way to heaven. Consequently, little emphasis was placed on the study of this world or on improving the conditions of life. The truly religious were expected to spend their time in worship, meditation and prayer. Most common folk, however, were not primarily interested in salvation. They were concerned with the problems of their everyday lives: sickness, plagues, famine, wars and uncertainty. To deal with these, many turned to Mary and the saints as intermediaries, and to diviners, witch doctors, medicine men and other practitioners of their pre-Christian past. Others, particularly those without social roots in stable communities, flocked to faith healers who promised them health and success.[2]

The Reformers rejected this wedding of animism and Christianity and stressed the active presence of God in the lives of people here and now.[3] They preached a strong theology of providence—of God as Lord not only of cosmic history, but also of human history and of personal biography.

However, the Renaissance which followed distorted the Reformation worldview by reintroducing a neoplatonic dualism into Western thought. Instead of the biblical worldview, in which the central distinction is between God the Creator and his creation, the neoplatonic worldview drew a sharp line between spirit and matter (Figure One). God, angels and demons were put together in the world of spiritual beings. Humans, animals, plants and matter were seen as "nature."

Modern Dualism

This shift at the worldview level led to our modern Western worldview that draws a sharp line between the "supernatural" and the "natural." The former has to do with otherworldly concerns, such as God, Satan, heaven, hell, sin, salvation, prayer and miracles. Nature—the world of matter, space and time—was increasingly seen as an autonomous realm operating according to natural laws that could be understood by scientists and used to solve human problems on this earth.

At first, scientists, working within a Christian worldview, saw God as the ultimate source and sustainer of the universe, but as science explained more and more in terms of "natural laws," many scientists believed they had no need for God to account for what they observed. The two worlds became divorced from each other and met only at creation, when God made matter and set the laws of nature in motion; and in miracles, when God "intervened" in nature and overrode natural laws. This had a powerful secularizing effect on Western thought.

Figure One
The Rise of the Modern Western Worldview

The Biblical Worldview	The Modern Neoplatonic Worldview

GOD THE CREATOR

-creates
-sustains

CREATION
-spirits
-humans
-animals
-plants
-matter

SUPERNATURAL WORLDS
(Domain of Religion)
-God, angels, Satan,
        demons
-creation, miracles, prayer
-related to ultimate
        questions

(little or no connection)

NATURAL WORLD
(Domain of Science)
-material world, humans,
        animals and plants
-natural laws, human
        control

By the twentieth century, there was little room for God in the Western worldview. The origins of the universe had been pushed back to a remote time, and scientists could now explain much that had been thought miraculous. God was needed only to account for what was unknown, and there was a deep faith that, given time, science would be able to explain even that.

Modern Dualism and Christianity

The modern neoplatonic dualism has left many western Christians with a spiritual schizophrenia. On the one hand, they believe in God and the cosmic history of creation-fall-redemption-final judgment. This provides them with ultimate meaning and purpose in life. On the other hand, they live in an ordinary world explained in naturalistic terms in which there is little room for God. They drive cars, use electricity and take medicines, all of which are the products of scientific understandings and reinforce a scientific way of thinking.

This internal tension is accentuated when Christians read the Bible. There they find God at work in human history with no sharp distinction made between natural and supernatural phenomena. The biblical worldview does not fit with modern secular explanations that deny spiritual realities, particularly in everyday experiences.

The consequences of this modern dualism in the church have been destructive. Liberal theologians sought to reduce the tension by explaining the miracles of the Bible totally in naturalistic terms. Conservative theologians affirmed the reality of miracles but often accepted a naturalistic view of the world. Many of them drew a line between "evangelism" and the "social gospel," thereby reinforcing the dualism that had led to the secularization of the West. For them, evangelism had to do with the supernatural salvation of the soul. The social gospel involved ministry to human bodily needs, such as food, medicine and education. This they dismissed as of secondary importance.

The Deification of the Self

A second consequence of the modern worldview was to place humans at the top of nature. With God out of the picture, humans became the gods of the earth. During the Renaissance, Machiavelli took the next logical step and called people to forget about salvation, which by his day had lost much of its clarity and urgency. Rather, he said, they should focus on enjoying life here on earth, which is real and immediate. Personal health, comfort and prosperity became the central goals of Western culture, and science the means to achieve them.

Left alone, however, modern humans faced a crisis of meaning. Now they were gods, but what kind of gods were they? Mechanistic science enabled humans to control nature, but it also gave them the power to destroy nature through violence, nuclear holocausts, chemical pollution and deforestation. The same science, applied to humans themselves, saw them as animals ruled by needs and irrational drives (Freudian psychology), as stimulus-response machines (behavioral psychology), or as robots programmed by their societies and cultures (sociology and anthropology). God was gone, but so was the human soul. There was no real meaning left in human life.

To recover a sense of meaning, western philosophers coined the term "self" to replace the concept of the "soul." It was assumed that people are autonomous selves and that, because they are now the gods, their individual well-being is the highest good.[4] This view of humans as independent, self-reliant selves was a radical shift from the biblical and medieval view of them as created in the image of God and dependent upon God at every moment for their existence and meaning.

Replacing "soul" with "self," however, did not solve the problem. The question now arose, what is this "self"? Some, such as Locke and Descartes, believed that it is reason. Humans are different from animals because they think, and using reason, they can create a happy, peaceful and meaningful world. Others, such as Rousseau and Nietzsche, disagreed. They believed that what makes humans different from animals and their lives meaningful is their ability to feel, to envision better worlds and to create them. Humans are culture builders. They are moral beings who find meaning in realizing their dreams about themselves. Both groups, however, agreed on one thing: meaning is to be found in self-fulfillment, in the good life here and now. The existential present, not eternity, is of primary importance.

This focus on the self became the dominant theme in western society during the last decade of the nineteenth century. The traditional Protestant values of salvation, the moral life, a life of work, saving and sacrifice, civic responsibility and self-denial for the good of others were replaced by a new set of values: personal realization, health, material comfort, immediate gratification and periodic leisure.[5] These, it was believed, could be achieved through buying material goods (largely on credit) and accumulating wealth. The gospel of self-indulgence was preached by a host of advertisers. Marlborough cigarettes free us from the drudgery of city life and put us out in Wyoming, with its clean air, stars and the thrill of the range. Coke, we are told, is the real thing.

This focus on the self was reinforced by Abraham Maslow, Fritz Perls, Carl Rogers and other key figures in the fledgling field of humanistic psychology. While they sought to restore human dignity, they did so by offering a psychology that glorified the self.

The result of this shift in the modern worldview is an almost obsessive concern with psychic and physical health. Life owes us comfort, health, happiness, success, prosperity and intense, ecstatic experiences. Failure, loss of self-worth and boredom, rather than sin, have become the implacable enemies, and therapy, consumption and miraculous cures the means of salvation. A new Western religion has emerged that offers us meaning based on self-realization, not forgiveness of personal sins and reconciliation with God and others.[6] Self has become god and self-fulfillment the ultimate goal. Personal biography has replaced cosmic history as the framework in which human significance is to be found. The only story most North Americans feel a part of is their own.[7]

The new gospel had a strong influence on Protestant Christianity, particularly the liberal wing. G. Stanley Hall asserted that the kingdom of God exalted "man here and now." Harry Emerson Fosdick and Norman Vincent Peale provided religious sanctions for the emerging value system. The starting point of Christianity, Fosdick claimed, was not an otherworldly faith, but a faith in human personality: "Not an outward temple, but the inward shrine of man's personality, with all its possibilities and powers, is . . . infinitely sacred."[8]

Bruce Barton reinterpreted Jesus in terms of the ideals of abundant vitality and intense experience. Barton's Jesus personified personal magnetism, vibrant health and outdoor living. He was no weak Lamb of God. Women adored him, and he was the most popular dinner guest in Jerusalem. "He did not come to establish a theology but to lead a life," Barton wrote. "Living more healthfully than any of his contemporaries, he spread health wherever he went . . . ." He offered righteousness as the path to "a happier, more satisfying way of living."[9] Health was no longer seen, along with sickness and suffering, as part of the human condition within God's greater plan of salvation or as a means by which God works out his purposes. It had become an end in itself, cloaked with religious value, something humans could and should strive to achieve.

This emphasis on self and the present has led to the North American individualism and pragmatism that emphasize short term personal problem-solving rather than ultimate meaning and truth. Self-realization, in one form or another, has become the dominant religion of the West.

Individualism and the Church

The effects of individualism on the Western church have been profound. Salvation increasingly has become a personal matter between the self and God, and has little to do with the formation of a new community in Christ. Many churches have become little more than religious clubs, organized on the basis of voluntary association and common interests. The relationship between members is no longer seen as sacrament (ordained of God) or covenant (commitment to a group) but contract (based on personal convenience). It should not surprise us, therefore, that Christians often do not find a congregation to be a true community or that they drift from church to church.

The deification of self is also beginning to make inroads into the church. More and more we hear the good news that we can have health, wealth and prosperity here and salvation in the life to come, and that without suffering, persecution, a cross or a sense of sin. An example of this comes from Rev. Ewing, in the introduction to his book, *If You Want **Money**, A Home in Heaven, Health and Happiness, Based on the Holy Bible, Do These Things* . . . . Ewing writes,

> This book is designed to **teach you** about the power that you have within you which can lift you up **from the midst of sickness, feeling down, failure, poverty** and **frustration,** and set you on the exciting road **to health, happiness, abundance** and **security.** I have seen miraculous transformations

take place in men and women from all walks of life when they begin releasing the power of faith that is within them and **sowing faith seeds**[10] (emphasis in the original).

The titles of the first four chapters are "You can have the desires of your heart," "God wants you to have plenty of money," "God wants to heal you everywhere you hurt" and "God will get you that good job you desire." This, of course, is an extreme case of the health and prosperity gospel, but it illustrates the fundamental assumptions of this theology, which is increasingly heard to some degree or another in the media and in churches.

II. THE COLLAPSE OF THE MODERN WORLDVIEW

Despite the physical well-being made possible by science, there is a growing doubt that this alone makes sense out of life or that science is the savior people once believed it would be. Even in the scientific world, many are beginning to reject the neoplatonic dualism that divorces spiritual realities from material ones and ultimate concerns from those of this life.[11] Increasingly there are calls for a post-modern worldview characterized by some type of holism that sees humans and the world as integrated and takes spiritual needs seriously. But what shape should it take? There are a number of worldviews competing for the post-modern mind.

The Return of Animism

Some leaders are promoting a return to the animistic beliefs that characterized much of the world before the rise of science—a world in which most things that happen are brought about, whimsically and arbitrarily, by spirits, ancestors, ghosts, magic, witchcraft and the stars. It is a world in which God is distant and in which humans are at the mercy of good and evil powers and must defend themselves by means of prayers and chants, charms, medicines and incantations. Power, not truth, is the central human concern in this worldview.

Such beliefs, suppressed during the reign of science, had never fully left the western mind. Below the level of orthodox Christianity, an assortment of folk religious beliefs have persisted, handed down by word of mouth, despite the opposition of church leaders and the ridicule of scientists. Samples of it can be seen in the tabloids sold in supermarkets and in stories of ghosts, witchcraft, evil eye and prophecies passed along as gossip.

Recently in mainstream North America there has been a resurgence of interest in the animistic worldview. The Saturday morning children's cartoons are full of supermen, witches, little people of various sorts, magic, curses and transformations. In movies and TV sitcoms exorcisms, black magic, spirits and resurrections are now commonplace. Similar themes appear in games such as "Dungeons and Dragons" and in rock music. These ideas may be presented as fiction, satire, humor or horror, but to those without a clear conceptual framework with which to test reality, the very presence of these ideas opens the door of doubt and later may lead to the acceptance of their reality.

More disturbing is the resurgence of serious pagan and occult practices in the West. As the Christian belief that humans are created in the image of God fades in Western thought, there has been a revival of pre-Christian paganism that puts humans in the same category with all other natural phenomena. All of these are at the mercy of capricious, invisible spirits and forces. The only human defense is to gain power over these spirits and forces by means of rituals and magic. Fertility rites, white witchcraft, divination, palmistry, fortune-telling and astrology are gaining credibility and acceptance in cities. Many bookshops now have sections set aside for the occult.

At the center of animism is the shaman, the religious practitioner who is a master of ecstasy, healing, prophecy and dealing with the spirit world.[12] The shaman seeks power through a personal encounter with a spirit. By means of trances in which the shaman visualizes hidden realities, and by means of guided imagery, he or she transforms these realities using invisible, personalized energy, performing miraculous cures and predicting future events.[13]

This resurgence of animistic thinking has influenced some in the church. The earlier denial of Satan and demons by some Christians is replaced by teachings that evil spirits and spirit possesions are common and account for much of what happens to Christians and non-Christians alike. The indirect source of many of these teachings is Kabala, the syncretistic Jewish folk religion that arose during the exile in Babylonia.

There is a two-fold danger in this return to an animistic worldview. First, it assigns too much power and authority to unseen spirits and forces in this world and implicitly denies the power and presence of God in everyday affairs, particularly in the lives of Christians. Humans must live in constant fear of capricious beings. The fact is that, when compared to pagan mythologies such as the Babylonian creation myths, the scriptures are remarkably secular. They speak of a divinely ordained and maintained natural order. They do affirm the realities of angels and demons, but humans are not the puppets of their capricious whims. The real focus of the Bible is the story of humans and their response to God. Moreover, in the end, it was normal human beings and their religious systems that crucified Christ, not those who were demon possessed. The universal testimony of animists who have responded to the gospel is that Christ has delivered them from their fear of demons.

Secondly, the animistic worldview rejects the insights of science. While modern scientists often reject God, science itself emerged within the context of a Christian worldview.[14] Many early scientists were Christians seeking to understand the order God placed in his creation (Genesis 1-2:4). To deny this order is to deny that the world and its history have meaning.

Birth of the New Age Movement

A second response to the collapse of Greek dualism in Western thought is the rise of the New Age movement. This is a collection of cults and teachings such as ESP, transcendental meditation, Church of Religious Science, Hari Krishna and other neo-Hindu religions, the new physics, New Age politics and New Age versions of Christianity.[15] Among its prophets are Shirley MacLaine, John Denver, Teilhard de Chardin, Maharishi Mahesh Yogi, Fritjof Capra and Carlos Castaneda.

As diverse as these are, underlying them is a convergence of teachings rooted in Eastern mysticism.[16] First, they affirm that "all is one." Ultimately there is no difference between spirit and matter, God and creation, good and evil, and one person and another. All belong to one interrelated, interdependent and interpenetrating reality that has no boundaries and no ultimate divisions. This is radically at odds with a Christian view of reality that affirms the difference between God and his creation, between sin and righteousness, and between facts and figments of human imagination.

A second premise of New Age is that all is God. This is a short step from declaring that all is one. But if all is God, then God is no longer a person in relationship to other beings and things. God is an impersonal energy, force or consciousness—an "it." This, of course, denies the personal nature of God as Creator and Lord.

A third teaching is that we are, in fact, gods. If God is all and all is God, then we too are part of divinity. We are not sinners in need of salvation; we are ignorant of our true selves and need enlightenment. We must discover that we ourselves are God by experiencing a new consciousness of cosmic reality. Self and self-realization become the measure and goal of religious experience; and self-realization can be achieved by exercising the hidden powers within us, the same powers that underlie the universe. Gone are the biblical teachings of sin and salvation, of love, reconciliation, fellowship and self-sacrifice, and of worship and submission to God.

A fourth belief shared by New Age movements is that reality is governed not by God nor by natural forces he has created, but by spiritual forces we can control once we are enlightened. It is we who control our own destiny. By imaging, mind control and faith we can make things happen. But we must experience the consciousness that enables us to see things as they really are. This altered state of consciousness can be reached through transcendental meditation, chanting, dancing, yoga, self-hypnotism, internal visualization, biofeedback or even sexual intercourse. Only then will we be freed from the tyranny of Western rationalism and materialism.

The final affirmation of New Age is that all religions are one and all lead to the truth. Jesus, Buddha, Lao-Tse, Krishna, Maharishi Mahesh Yogi and others are enlightened gurus that can lead us to experience our oneness with each other and with the universe.

Christ is not the only way, and there is no place for evangelism. Salvation lies within each of us.

Central to New Age is its promise of holistic health. If the mind can control reality, there is no need for anyone to be sick, poor or unsuccessful. The solution to our problems lies within us, in our mindset, in our faith. New Age claims to treat not only the sickness, but the whole person—body, mind and spirit—by meditation, visualization, biofeedback, psychic healing, transpersonal psychology, guidance by a "spirit guide" and often folk healers.[17] Death itself is viewed as a transition to another state of consciousness.

This new view of the world, which has its roots in Hinduism, is spreading rapidly in Europe and North America because it promises to fulfill the western search for personal well-being and success. It promises a "New Age" of hope and human fulfillment. Its approach to Christianity is one of subversion. Its promise of spiritual power and ecstasy attracts many Christians unaware of its theological foundations.[18]

III. A THEOLOGY OF GOD'S WORK IN OUR EVERYDAY LIVES

What alternative do we as Christians have to the worldviews offered by consumerism, animism and New Age, all of which deify the self? What criteria do we use to test new movements such as the current emphasis on healing and exorcisms so as not to become captive to the spirit of our times as has happened to Christians so often in the past? It is important that Christianity stands in prophetic critique of the times in which we live, that we not allow it to become just another version of the West's preoccupation with success, health and the present. To guard against this, we must formulate clear theological guidelines rooted in scripture. To chart a course through the turbulent seas of our times, we need a theology of healing, exorcism, provision and guidance. Such a theology, dealing with God's work in our daily lives, must be part of our broader theological understandings of God, creation, sin, cross, judgment and redemption. Furthermore, in such a theology we must reject the old dualism that confines God's work to other-

Figure Two
A Trinitarian View of God's Work in the World Today

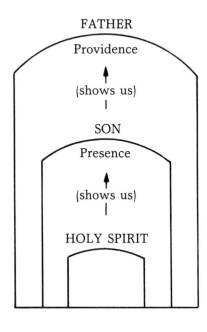

FATHER	-maintains creation
	-superintends history
SON	-victory on the cross
	-sustains us in trials
	-our exemplar in incarnation and servanthood
HOLY SPIRIT	-gives us victory
	-manifests signs of the kingdom

worldly concerns and leaves him out of our everyday lives except for an occasional miracle.

What are some of the theological guidelines that can help us discover again how God wants to work in our personal lives?

A Trinitarian Theology

A theology of God's work in human affairs must begin with an understanding of God himself—as Father, Son and Holy Spirit (see Figure Two). Often new movements in the church focus their attention on one person in the Godhead and so lose sight of the work of the others.

The Providence of the Father. Throughout the scriptures, it is clear that God is sovereign over the ebb and flow of history. From creation to final judgment, God is in control. This does not deny humans their freedom to make choices. It does, however, mean that in the end God directs the overall course of history according to his purposes. Moreover, the scriptures are clear that God is concerned about the life of each person, including the smallest of details.

For the early Christians, the ongoing involvement of God in world history and in personal biography was a living reality. This awareness guided their lives and sustained them in times of persecution and martyrdom. In fact, more often than not, following Christ meant suffering, sickness and death, rather than health, prosperity and long life. This awareness also gave them answers to the problems of daily living.

Following Constantine, Christianity became identified with government, and God was seen as a distant ruler associated with the religious and political elite. By the Middle Ages, the common folk no longer saw God as involved in their daily lives, so they took their troubles to the saints: to St. Anthony when something was lost, to St. Peregrinus Laziosi for cancer and to St. Luke for other diseases. They also used magical chants, charms and potions to guard themselves against sickness and danger.

The Reformation not only recovered the biblical understanding of salvation, but also restored the doctrine of providence. Calvin, Luther, Zwingli and the other Reformers declared that God is indeed the God of history, both individual and collective. He does not leave his people to fend for themselves in a world of chance and happenstance, nor does he delegate ordinary human affairs to angels and saints. He himself as Father cares for their everyday lives. It was this profound faith that God is the God of human and personal as well as cosmic history that gave the Reformation much of its power. Over time, however, this living awareness of God's superintending presence faded, and the doctrine of providence became largely a theological postulate.

The most significant defect in John Wimber's teaching, according to Wallace Benn and Mark Burkill, is his failure to appreciate the sovereignty of God and its implications.[19] There is little recognition that it may be God's will for a Christian to be sick or suffer or that God can use these for their good. There is little recognition of the fact that illnesses are often the body's warning that people are living unhealthy lifestyles. There is little acknowledgement that in many areas of life Christians and non-Christians share equally in the common lot of fallen humanity. Together they suffer because of earthquakes, famines, plagues and ordinary human sickness. This does not mean that God is uninterested in the lot of Christians. It does mean that he loves both the saved and the lost and that he is working out his purposes within a fallen world and will one day deliver his people from it.

Today we need to recover the doctrine of providence as a living reality in our everyday lives, for it is the encompassing frame within which we must understand all human experiences. God is the God of history: of Russia, China and India as well as of North America and Europe. And God is the God of our lives: of sickness, pain, failure, oppression and death as well as of healing, joy and success. He uses all these for our ultimate good (Romans 8:28). In times of difficulty, we may doubt God's providence. We do not always feel his hand in ours. But later, in retrospect, we realize that God was closest to us in our times of trial.

The Presence of the Son. Within this bigger frame, we need to experience the presence of the living Christ with us. As humans, we live in a world suffering the consequences of the fall. Plagues, famines, wars, suffering and death are part of our human experience (Rom. 8:19-23). As Christians living in a fallen world, we can expect hardships, poverty and persecution (I Cor. 4:10-13; II Tim. 3:12; I Peter 4:12-18). Moreover, we are called to take up our cross and follow Christ (Matt. 10:38-39; 16:24-26). The good news is that in all of these experiences Christ is with us (Matt. 28:7).

This presence manifests itself first in our salvation. It was Christ whose death and resurrection made salvation possible. That salvation is also at work in us today. Christ saved us and is saving us from the power and judgment of sin.

This presence is found in the fact that the Master who once walked the lanes of Galilee is the same Master who is invisibly present with us (Matt. 28:20). There is nothing that can separate us from his love and care (Rom. 8:35-39). The Father answers our prayers because Christ pleads for us (John 14-15). And Christ provides us with the grace and strength to live with "weaknesses, insults, hardships, persecutions and calamities" (II Cor. 12:10).

This presence is seen in the reality of the church, which is Christ's body. As John Bright points out, "It is a pitiful and helpless minority composed, for the most part, of people of no account (cf. I Cor. 1:26-28), the offscouring and disinherited."[20] Nevertheless, it has turned the world upside down.

Finally, this presence is found in the hope of our future resurrection—a hope founded on the resurrection of Christ himself and promised to us who believe (I Cor. 15).

This was the message of the sixteenth-century Anabaptists, with their emphasis on living moment by moment in fellowship and obedience to Christ. Later, when the Reformation doctrine of providence was reduced to scholastic debates, it became the message of the Pietists. Today it is the message of the East African revival, whose emphasis on "living in the light" has sustained the church in Uganda in some of the most terrible persecutions in history. It is a message we must recover.

The Power of the Spirit. The Pentecostals and charismatics remind us that within the care of the Father and the presence of Christ we need to experience the power of the Holy Spirit. This power was demonstrated in the life of Christ and in the early church in signs and wonders. But, as Paul, Peter, John and the other writers of the New Testament point out in their theological reflections, such demonstrations are secondary to the power of the Holy Spirit within humans, leading them to salvation and to a victorious life in Christ.

The power of the Holy Spirit is at work first in convicting people of their sins and wooing them to faith in Christ. Without the Spirit, there can be no faith.[21] On the other hand, we receive the Spirit when we respond in faith to the gospel. To be more specific than this only leads to endless quibbling about the order of Christian experience. Denny notes,

> The faith which abandons itself to Christ is at the same time a receiving of the Spirit of Christ . . . . There are not two things here but one, though it can be represented in the two relations which the words faith and Spirit suggest. Where human responsibility is to be emphasized, it is naturally faith which is put to the front (Gal. 3:2); where the gracious help of God is the

main point, prominence is given to the Spirit.[22]

Not only does the Holy Spirit play an important role in bringing us to salvation, but he also gives us the assurance of that salvation (Rom. 8:14; I John 3:24).

Secondly, the Holy Spirit leads us into the truth (John 14:17). Without his ongoing work in us, we cannot comprehend the mysteries of the gospel. Before his departure, Jesus promised to send to his followers the Spirit of Truth (John 16:1-3; see also I John 5:7). He also referred to the Spirit as the Counselor who would convince the world concerning sin and righteousness and judgment (John 14:25; 16:8).

Thirdly, the Spirit transforms our lives (II Cor. 3:18). He enables us to have victory over sin (Eph. 6:17). He helps us in our weaknesses (Rom. 8:26). He sensitizes our consciences (Rom. 9:1). He sanctifies us and makes us holy (I Cor. 6:11; I Peter 1:2). He strengthens us and comes to our aid in moments of crisis (Eph. 3:16; Mark 13:11; Luke 12:12). And the Spirit will resurrect our mortal bodies from death just as he raised Christ from the dead (Rom 8:11).

Fourthly, the power of the Holy Spirit is manifest in the preaching and persuasion of the gospel. Christ himself was anointed by the Spirit to preach the Good News (Luke 4:18-19). Paul repeatedly connects *pneuma* (Spirit) and *dunamis* (power) in contexts which deal with the missionary preaching of the apostles. He writes, "For our gospel came to you not only in word, but also in power and in the Holy Spirit and with full conviction . . . . For you received the word in much affliction, with joy inspired by the Holy Spirit" (I Thess. 1:5-6).

There is a danger here of equating "power" with "miracles." For example, John Wimber writes in *Power Evangelism*, "When first-century Christians came to a new town signs and wonders followed."[23] He concludes, "Signs and wonders resulted in dramatic church growth. They were the catalyst for evangelism."[24] The fact is that few who were healed became disciples. The power of the Holy Spirit is manifest in the gospel itself, which is the power of God unto salvation (Rom. 1:6), and in the cross, which is foolishness to the world (I Cor. 1:18). Paul reminds us that "faith comes from what is heard, and what is heard comes by the preaching of Christ'' (Rom. 10:17).

The Whole Work of God. The activities of the Father, Son and Holy Spirit are not three separate works. They are the work of one God. We are often most aware of the Holy Spirit in our lives here and now, for it is his task to lead us day by day. The task of the Holy Spirit (who is also called the Spirit of Christ in Romans 8:9) is to point us to Jesus Christ and not to himself (John 14:26; 16:13-15). He is God at work within us, leading us to glorify and obey Christ as Lord.

Christ's work, on the other hand, is to reveal to us the Father and to glorify him on earth (John 17). It is in Christ that we humans see the definitive revelation of the nature and being of God the Father (John 14:9-11).

The Father's work is to send the Spirit and to exalt Christ, so that at his name every knee shall one day bow, in heaven, on earth and under the earth (Phil. 2:10-11).

If we overlook the whole work of God on earth and focus on only a part, or if we ignore the central thrust of God's purposes, we are in danger of distorting the truth.

A Theology of Creation and Redemption

In developing a theology of God's work in our everyday lives, we must reject the modern dualism that restricts God to otherworldly matters and leaves the natural world to science. We must begin with a theology of creation, God's first act, in order to understand what were God's original and ultimate purposes. It is within that framework that we must locate our theology of redemption, in which God restores his creation ruined by sin. In eternity, God's perfect creation, redeemed through Christ, will continue, but God's redemptive acts will then be in the past.

In developing a theology of creation and redemption, we must see God at work in cosmic history (in creation, fall, redemption and eternity), in human history (in the affairs of nations and individuals to bring about his cosmic purposes) and in natural history (in the material order he created, which also awaits redemption) (Rom. 8:22; II Peter 3:11-13; see Figure Three). We are taught the first of these in our churches, but often we explain human and natural

Figure Three
God's Work in this World

GOD
involved in: answers the questions of:

COSMIC HISTORY	-ultimate origin, purpose and destiny of the universe, societies and individuals
HUMAN HISTORY	-the meaning of life and death -human well-being and natural suffering, including sickness, famine, barrenness, earthquakes, etc. -guidance in the face of the unknown and the uncertainties of the future -success and the fear of failure
NATURAL HISTORY	-the natural order and its service to humans -the sociocultural orders and their relationship to the kingdom of God

history in secular terms and thereby reinforce the neoplatonic dualism that underlies modern thought. Only as we bring God back into the very center of history and science will we root out the secularism that has plagued our age.

It is not easy for us, however, to return to such a holistic theology. Many of our words in English contain an implicit neoplatonic dualistic worldview. For example, we speak of "supernatural" in contrast to "natural" and "miracle" in contrast to "ordinary" or "normal." But these reflect a nonbiblical worldview. The term "nature," which implies an autonomous, self-sustained universe, is not found in Hebrew thought. Rather, the word used for this world and its order is *bara*, "what is created." The term, in fact, is a verb and implies an origin in and continued dependence on God. To us, some events may seem ordinary and others extraordinary. In fact, all are due to the active, sustaining hand of God. In the biblical sense, no birth of a child is "natural," nor any divine healing "unnatural" in the sense of being contrary to the divinely created order.

Therefore we first need to see all healing as God's work. If we place too much emphasis on "miraculous" healing, we are in danger, in the long run, of reinforcing secularism. To overstress the miraculous implies that what is not miraculous is "natural" and can be explained without God. It puts what the church does through prayer in opposition to what humans can do by modern scientific medicine in hospitals. To non-Christians, the latter far outweighs what the church can show. Christians often turn to medicine when their prayers fail. The dichotomy is false to begin with. God works in both ordinary and extraordinary ways.

Secondly, a focus on miracles as the key evidence of God at work in our lives leaves us essentially with a God-of-the-gaps. We use him to acount for what science cannot. But as science makes new discoveries, it often explains in "ordinary" terms what we once reserved for the miraculous. For instance, Christians once prayed for protection from lightning; now they put up lightning rods and no longer pray. The error here is to see God chiefly at work in the miraculous. We must see his hand as much in what we think we understand as in what we do not.

Thirdly, as we will see later, miracles are reported in all religions. Scripture itself warns us that Satan will perform them (II Thess. 2:9). In other words, miracles are not self-authenticating; they themselves must be tested to determine their source.

When we are new in faith, it is natural for us to look for visible evidences of God's existence, such as healings and material blessings. As we grow in faith, we root our faith in God's revelation of himself through the scriptures and in our personal walk with him. We also begin to see his hand as much in the miracle of a child or a tree as in a vision, in the "ordinary" recovery of the body tended by a doctor as in a dramatic "extraordinary" healing.

A Theology of the Kingdom of God

Within a theology of creation, we need a theology of the kingdom of God, particularly as this has to do with God's work in the world after the fall. Sickness, suffering, starvation and death—these are the consequences of sin. Christ's response was to come as a human in order to establish and proclaim his kingdom as the new work of God on earth. This is what he preached (Matt. 4:23; Mark 1:14). It is the message of salvation that includes good news to the poor, release to the captives, sight to the blind and liberty to the oppressed (Luke 4:18-19). But how does the kingdom of God relate to our experiences as we continue to live in the kingdoms of this world: to famines, oppression, poverty, suffering, disease and death?

Down through history there have been prophets who claimed that the kingdom of God has already come in its fullness for God's people.[25] Christians, they said, need not be sick or poor or failures or sinners—or even die. This, in fact, was a heresy in Paul's day, when some claimed that the resurrection had already come for God's people (II Tim. 2:18). In recent years we see a resurgence of this message, which fits well with our western cultural emphasis on ourselves and our health, wealth and success, and our denial of death.[26] Despite such preaching, sincere, devout, praying Christians remain poor and broken. They become sick and die.

The kingdom of God *has come to us* in the person of Christ. It is found wherever God's people are obedient to the King. But the kingdom will come *in its fullness* only with Christ's return (Rev. 12:10). Until then, we live, as it were, between two worlds. We are people of this sinful world: we are tempted and sin; we are weak and we fall; and the processes of degeneration and death are at work in us from the moment of our birth. But we are also people of the kingdom: though we sin, in God's sight we are sinless; we face death, but we have eternal life; we see a decaying world around us, but we also see the signs of a heavenly kingdom in the transformed lives of God's people.

"Signs and wonders" is the phrase used in scripture for self-authenticating demonstrations of supernatural power. The phrase, however, is ambiguous. At times it points to the acts of God (Acts 2:22,43). At other times it refers to the works of false prophets. Bright notes,

> In the language of the Synoptic Gospels, at least, the miracles of Christ are never spoken of as "signs and wonders" *(se-meia kai terata)*, i.e., self-authenticating exhibitions of divine power designed to prove the claims of Jesus in the eyes of the people. Indeed, such "signs" (i.e., marvels) were precisely the sort of thing Christ refused to perform (e.g., Mark 8:11-12; Matt. 12:38-40). False messiahs are the ones who show off with "signs and wonders" (Mark 13:22; Matt. 24:24), and for Jesus to have done likewise would have been, from that point of view at least, the flat disproof of his claim to be the true Messiah. On the contrary, his miracles are "mighty works" ("powers," *dunameis*) of the kingdom of God.[27]

There are a number of misunderstandings regarding these terms against which we must guard. First, signs and wonders should not be simply equated with miracles. The terms refer to anything that reminds us that God is with us, "miraculous" or not. The rainbow is the sign of God's covenant with Noah (Gen. 9:12), circumcision the sign of his covenant with Israel (Gen. 17:11), Moses' mighty works signs of God's deliverance of his oppressed people (Ex. 4:17) and the Sabbath a sign of God's covenant with his people. Isaiah walked barefoot as a sign of God's judgment on Egypt and Ethiopia (Is. 20:3), and the sun went back ten "steps" as a sign of God's healing of Hezekiah (II Kings 20:9-11). Similarly, in the New Testament, the fact that Christ was wrapped in swaddling clothes and lying in a manger was a sign to the shepherds that this was the Messiah (Luke 2:12), and Judas' kiss a sign that this man was Jesus (Matt. 26:48).

Nor should signs and wonders be associated only with God. Pharaoh's magicians did signs (Ex. 7:10-22), and so do Satan (II Thess. 2:9) and false prophets (Matt. 24:24). They are not proofs of God's presence—they themselves need to be tested for their source. A sign is anything that reminds us of something else, an event that points beyond itself.

Secondly, signs and wonders that come from God should not be equated with the coming of the kingdom *in its fullness*. Rather, they are promises, reassuring us that the kingdom indeed will come (Rom. 8:22-25; II Cor. 5:1-5). They themselves are not that kingdom—they point to it and show us something of its nature. From time to time God does heal our physical diseases to enable us to do his work and to show us the nature of the kingdom, but the fullness of health will come only with our new bodies beyond death. To claim that Christians should never be ill or that when they are sick God will always heal them is to declare that the kingdom of God has come to them in its fullness. But this denies that death is still at work within them, and it settles for much too little. In the kingdom yet to come we will not just have our present bodies, healthy and strong—we will have new bodies that transcend anything we can imagine.

Thirdly, signs and wonders are not ends in themselves. Their purpose is to convey God's message to us. As David Hubbard notes, "The primary motive for divine miracle is not compassion but revelation"—or, one might say, God's mighty works are a revelation of divine compassion (cf. Ps. 107). Throughout scripture God performs miracles at critical junctures in history and in the lives of his people. He delivered Israel from Egypt, he defeated their enemies when they were outnumbered, and he spoke to them when they had forgotten him by messages and miracles through Elijah and Elisha. He announced by signs that Jesus was indeed the Messiah, the Christ. Today some turn to God because of a special work he has performed in their lives at their moment of decision. Others experience his presence in particular ways in moments of crisis and despair.

One common temptation is to focus on the signs themselves rather than on the message they bear (cf. John 6:26; Luke 23:8-9). Many people want healing, but they are not willing to give up all to follow Christ. Like the rich young ruler, they want the blessings of living with Christ, but they do not want to hear him say, "Sell what you have and give it to the poor, and follow me" or "Whoever loses his life for my sake will find it." Nor are they happy when Paul reminds them that Christians are often called to bear persecution, including beatings, mutilations and other physical wounds, and that this suffering is an honor (Phil. 1:29). These are not words they want to hear in an age of self-fulfillment. The kingdom of God comes in signs, but one of these signs is suffering for the sake of Christ.

Another temptation is to confuse the sign with the reality. Those who do this are like the man on his way to San Francisco who saw a sign pointing the way and camped under it, thinking he had arrived.

A Theology of Power

Today in the church we hear calls for demonstrations of power. This should not surprise us, for power is the central concern of our day. Nor should it surprise us that some see divine power as the key to prosperity, to health, to overcoming opposition and, above all, to controlling their own lives.

The scriptures have much to say about power. God is the God Almighty (*El Shaddai*, Gen. 17:1), who created and sustains all things by his power (Gen. 1), who defeated Satan and his hosts (John 16:33) and who will bring all things into subjection to himself (Eph. 1:22). Moreover, by his might he saved us and gave us the power to become like him in our lives and bear witness of his greatness. All this we must affirm.

Scripture also has much to say about the ways in which power is to be used. Unfortunately, many Christians think of power as the world around them does. They see it as active—it manifests itself by demonstrations of might that overcome the resistance of the opposition. Consequently, they seek to show the world God's superiority by means of power encounters that demonstrate his ability to heal and cast out demons, confident that when non-Christians see these, they will believe.

This, however, is not the picture we find in scripture or in history. There are demonstrations of God's power in preliminary confrontations of evil. Elijah called down fire from heaven, Jesus healed the sick and cast out demons, Peter and John healed the lame man at the temple gate, and Stephen, full of grace and power, did many signs and wonders among the people. These demonstrations, however, were not followed by mass conversions. Some believed, but then the opposition arose. Elijah fled to the desert and wrestled with depression as Jezebel appointed new prophets for Baal. Jesus and Stephen were arrested and killed. Peter and John were thrown into jail.

The history of such "power encounters" is that after the preliminary confrontation, "the powers" mobilize in opposition. These powers are Satan and his hosts. They are also human organizations—institutions, governments and societies—such as those that crucified Christ and persecuted the early church. Ever since Babel, the center of the opposition to the kingdom of God has been the organized systems of sane people in corporate rebellion against God. Our first sin as humans was self-deification. We wanted neither God nor Satan to lord it over us; we wanted to be our own gods. And the same is still true today.

God's supreme victory over Satan took place at the cross and the resurrection. Satan used his full might seeking to destroy Christ or to provoke him to use his divine might in response. Either would have meant defeat for Christ, the first because Satan would have overcome him and the second because it would have destroyed God's plan of salvation. Godly power is always rooted in love, not pride; redemption, not conquest; and concern for the other, not the self. It is humble, not proud, and inviting, not rejecting. Its symbol is the cross, not the sword. This is why to the world it is seen as weakness (I Cor. 1:23-27).

As Christians and as churches, we are in desperate need of showing God's power in transformed lives and in a Christlike confrontation of evil wherever we find it, whether demonic or systemic. We need also to guard against distortions of a biblical view of power. We must not look at power in worldly terms. Furthermore, we must not divorce power from truth. What we need, some say, is demonstrations of power, not theological reflection. But power is not self-authenticating—it must be tested for its source. Moreover, demonstrations of power seldom lead people to truth and salvation. Jesus healed many, but few of them became his disciples. Of the ten lepers he healed, one returned, and then only to give thanks.

Finally, we must guard against temptations to control power ourselves and so to make ourselves gods. The power God gives is never our own. We are simply stewards called to be faithful in using that power to the glory of God, not our own honor or advancement.

A Theology of Discernment

In dealing with divine healing and provision, we need a theology of discernment. Signs and wonders are not confined to Christianity. Miraculous healings, speaking in tongues, prophecies, resurrections and other extraordinary experiences are reported in all major religions. For example, Baba Farid, a Pakistani Muslim saint, is said to have cured incurable diseases, raised a dying man to life, converted dried dates into gold nuggets and covered vast distances in a moment.[28] Hundreds of thousands flock each year to the Hindu temple to Venkateswara at Tirupathi, south India, many of them fulfilling vows because they claim the god healed them when they prayed to him during their illnesses. Similar reports come from Buddhist temples in southeast Asia and spiritist shrines in Latin America. Yogis claim that they can rise from the dead and shamans report trips into heaven. Upwards of 15,000 people claim healing each year at Lourdes, and many more at the Virgin of Guadelupe near Mexico City. Healing is also central to Christian Science, and testimonies of miraculous healing are reported in every issue of the *Christian Science Sentinel.* One man wrote that he was healed from astigmatism after applying the principles taught by Mary Baker Eddy in *Science and Health with Key to the Scriptures.* Another wrote,

> I had two healings after I had attended the Sunday school for some time. One was a large birthmark on my forehead. The other was a severe skin condition . . . . Some later healings came quickly; others took longer and involved more study on my part, sometimes with help from a Christian Science practitioner. But I was always healed.[29]

In short, there is no *phenomenon* that in itself is proof of God's presence.

How are we to respond to all this? Scripture itself is clear that Satan performs signs and wonders, counterfeiting God's work. It warns us to guard against being led astray (Matt. 7:15-16; I Tim. 4:1,7; II Tim. 3:1-4:5; II Thess. 2:9-10). Nowhere are we encouraged to let our minds go blank in order to let the Holy Spirit come in. That is a technique commonly found in cults. Rather, we are to seek the wisdom that enables us to test the spirits to see whether or not they come from God (I Cor. 12:3; I Thess. 5:20-21; I John 4:1-6). In this, our attitude should not be one of skepticism but of openness to hearing the voice of God when he truly speaks to us.

What are the signs that enable us to discern the work of God and differentiate it from the work of self or Satan? It is too simple to say that what God's people do is of God (cf. Matt. 7:21-23) or that what non-Christians do is of Satan (cf. Num. 22-24).

Nor are physical phenomena the test of the work of the Holy Spirit. Many today, including Wimber, appeal to warm sensations, fluttering eyelids, involuntary muscle movements and feelings of "energy" coming into the body as proof that God is at work. Lloyd-Jones warns us that such experiences are common also in other religions. He writes,

> You will find in the case of spiritist healing that there is always emphasis on the physical element. People will testify to a feeling of heat as the hand of the healer came upon them, or of a sensation like an electric shock, or something like that—the physical is always very prominent . . . . There is nothing corresponding to that in the New Testament . . . . They do not talk much about their physical sensations but about the Lord and his love for them, and their love for him.[30]

Our experiences must themselves be tested, for they are not self-authenticating. We need to avoid reading our experiences into scripture and focusing on them rather than on the scripture itself.

Similarly, the "words of knowledge" widely used in many healing services need themselves to be tested. God warned Israel not to take prophesying lightly, for those who speak claim to speak for God (Deut. 13). Those whose prophecies did not come true were to be stoned. Those whose prophecies did come true but who led the people away from God were also condemned. Paul issues the same warning (I Cor. 12:3; I Thess. 5:20-21). Luke commends the church in Berea for testing Paul's teachings (Acts 17:11).

The Bible provides us with other tests. First, *does the teaching, practice or movement give glory to God rather than to humans* (John 7:18; 8:50; 12:27-28; 17:4)? Unfortunately, in extremely individualistic, culturally diverse societies such as we have in North America, people tend to follow strong personalities. Little other social cohesion brings them together into groups. We must be aware, therefore, of the particular temptation in our society to deify strong leaders.

Secondly, *does it recognize the lordship of Christ* (I John 2:3-5; 5:3; James 2:14-19)? The test here is not primarily one of orthodoxy, but of obedience. The question is not whether the leader and movement affirm the truth that Jesus is Lord or even that they feel a great love for him. The question is one of submission to Christ. In other words, there must be an attitude of humility, learning and willingness to obey.

Thirdly, *does a teaching, practice or movement conform to scriptural teaching?* Are those involved willing to submit their lives and teachings to the instruction of the scriptures and the leading of the Holy Spirit? This must be an ongoing process, for the scriptures provide the norm against which we must examine all doctrine.

Fourthly, *are the leaders of a movement accountable to others in the church?* The interpretation of scripture is, ultimately, not a personal matter but a concern of the church as a hermeneutical community.[31] We must test our understandings with others in leadership (Gal. 2:1-2) and with the teachings of the saints down through history. In an age of extreme individualism and a focus on great personalities, this test is of particular importance.

Fifthly, *do those involved manifest the fruit of the Spirit* (Gal. 5:22-25)? Is there love, or self-centeredness? Joy, or only excitement? Peace, or frenzy and tension? Patience, or short tempers? Gentleness, or arrogance? Goodness, or intrigue? Faith in God, or dependence on human planning? Meekness, or arrogance? And moderation, or excesses? Luther pointed out that the difference between Christians and pagan miracle workers is not the kinds of miracles they do, but in the transformations that take place in their lives. The power of God transforms us into the likeness of Christ; the powers of self and the world do not.

Sixthly, *does the teaching and practice lead us toward spiritual maturity* (I Cor. 12-14)? Some things are characteristic of spiritual immaturity, such as a dependence on miracles to reassure us that God indeed is and is with us. As we grow spiritually mature, we leave these things behind and root our faith in God himself, in his self-revelation to us through scripture and in a personal walk with him.

Seventhly, *is the truth kept in balance with other truths* (Matt. 23:23-24)? There are many teachings that are true, but to over or underemphasize them is error. It is wrong to take secondary truth and make it primary. For example, we can so emphasize peace or justice or healing or exorcisms or even salvation that in practice they become the whole of our gospel. It is Christ who is the center of the gospel, and when he is at the center, the many dimensions of the kingdom fall into their proper balance.

Finally, *does the teaching lead us to seek the unity of the body of Christ, or is it divisive* (John 17:11; I John 2:9-11; 5:1-2)? Love for one another is the hallmark of the church (John 5:12). This does not mean that divisions will not occur. It does mean that teachings that lead us to a sense of spiritual superiority have led us astray. We must work for fellowship and continued relationships with Christians who disagree with us and weep when they reject us or go astray.

A Theology of Suffering and Death

Finally, we need a theology of sickness, injury, suffering and death. These consequences of sin cannot be divorced from each other. The processes of aging and death are at work in humans from the moment of their conception. The side effects of this are sickness and bodily suffering. While God often does heal us by natural and by extraordinary means, our full delivery is only after death, when we receive our new body. For Christians, death is the final release, for we would not want to live forever in our present world, even in perfect health.

Here Wimber's teaching is particularly weak. He claims, "It's God's nature to heal not to teach us through sickness. Sickness is generally not beneficial."[32] To reconcile this position with scriptural teaching regarding suffering, Wimber must divorce sickness from bodily injuries suffered in persecution and from death, for the Bible makes clear that the latter are the lot of those who follow Christ (Heb. 11:35-38; Gal. 5:11; II Tim. 3:12). He says, "There is no indication in Scripture that suffering means or includes sickness."[33]

This denial that God can and does use sickness to teach us is hard to maintain on biblical grounds. Paul speaks of his "thorn in the flesh." Most Bible scholars agree that this was some normal bodily affliction or disease. Moreover, Paul refers to colleagues who were not healed (Phil. 2:26-27; I Tim. 4:20). Job too was sick, but God used everything that befell him to bring him to a more mature and deeper faith (Job 42:5-6).

It is also hard to maintain in terms of Christian experience. Many Christians testify to the fact that it was in times of sickness and suffering that they were drawn closest to Christ and learned important lessons of faith. Those are times when people realize their own vulnerability and their dependence on God.

Furthermore, it is hard to believe that God is more concerned about the illness of Christians in ordinary life than in the wounds and injuries of those who are suffering for the sake of Christ. Nowhere does Wimber take seriously the possibility that it may be God's will for a Christian to suffer.

A corollary of this is that for Christians, death is a defeat. This, in fact, is what Wimber claimed with regard to the death of David Watson, the British charismatic leader, despite repeated prayers for healing.[34] There is no place in Wimber's theology for seeing death as positive, as going to meet the Lord, or for godly dying, in which Christians look forward in peace to being with Christ and their departed loved ones. Certainly the power of the gospel is seen more clearly in our resurrection in a new life beyond than in the preservation of our lives here. Moreover, godly deaths have been powerful testimonies to the truth of the gospel and have led many to Christ.

Unfortunately, a theology that rejects sickness and suffering fits well into our age, with its denial of death[35] and emphasis on positive thinking.

IV. DANGERS

Like most movements in the church, the current emphasis on healing, prophecy and exorcism has both positive and negative sides to it. It reminds us of the need to take seriously the work of the Holy Spirit in meeting everyday human needs. It is in danger, however, of placing primary emphasis on what is of secondary importance in scripture and of bending the gospel to fit the spirit of our times. Satan often tempts us at the point of our greatest strengths. His method is not to sell us rank heresy, but to take the good we have and distort it by appealing to our self-interests (cf. Gen. 3). What are some of the dangers in the current emphasis on healing and exorcism against which we must guard?

Basing Theology on Experience

Living as we do in a culture based on pragmatism, it is easy for us to base our theology on experience. The test of truth is success. The sign of spiritual life and vital worship is feelings of excitement. The measure of our methods is growth and size.

In his evaluation of the great revivals of which he was a part, Jonathan Edwards cautioned against using experience to validate theology. Specifically, he gave twelve tests which were *not* signs of the work of God. Among them are:

• "Great religious experiences in themselves are no sign of their validity or that necessarily they are from God."
• "Religious experiences which have great effect upon the body are not necessarily valid."
• "Multiplied religious experiences, accompanying one another, are no evidence that the experience is necessarily saving or divine."
• "Spiritual experiences which stimulate the spending of much time in religious activity and zealous participation in the externals of worship are not necessarily saving experiences."
• "Religious experiences which cause men and women to praise and glorify God with their mouths are not necessarily saving and divine."[36]

In worship and in ministry we must test our human experiences against a theology based on biblical revelation, and guard lest we use those experiences to determine our theology.

Self-centeredness

We live in a modern society that places the self at the center of life. In such a setting, we need to guard against a theology that mirrors our times by focusing on ourselves and not on God and his agenda. The danger here is two-fold.

First, it is dangerously easy to institutionalize immaturity. New believers do indeed generally come to Christ with their own interests in mind—their salvation, their health, their well-being—and God begins with them where they are. The church must do the same. But God calls us to spiritual growth, in which our obsession with ourselves gives way to a love for God and others. Christian maturity is to imitate Christ, the person who lived for others. While ministering to seekers at their points of need, the primary focus should be on more mature expressions of worship and ministry.

Unfortunately, many Christians have bought into the western cultural emphasis on personal health and prosperity as ultimate ends in themselves. As a result, we focus on ourselves while millions around the world are dying of poverty, oppression and violence.

Health in scripture is defined, not in terms of personal well-being, but in terms of *shalom*, or loving relationships. It begins when we are reconciled to God and our enemies. It manifests itself in our mutual submission to one another in the church and our self-sacrificng service of others in need. Its fruit is physical and psychological health. To focus on personal well-being and prosperity rather than on *shalom* is to preach a gospel that treats the symptoms but does not cure the illness.

Secondly, it is a small but dangerous step from self-centeredness to self-deification. Ever since the Garden of Eden, this has been the first and most fundamental of human sins. Satan did not tempt Adam and Eve to worship him, but to worship themselves—their own freedom, their rights, their potential of becoming gods. Self-possession, not demon possession, is the greatest danger in our Western societies.

The results of this self-centeredness in the church can be devastating. It leads to spiritual pride: the feeling among those involved in a movement that they are spiritually superior to those who are not, and a judgmental attitude towards those who disagree with them. It also leads to competition for power and divisions in the church. Christ-centeredness, on the other hand, leads to humility, a desire for the unity of the church and a willingness to hear as well as to speak (Rom. 15:1-2; I Cor. 10:12).

Confusing Reports with Reality

Those who emphasize miraculous healing often base their claims on personal testimonies of those who have experienced healings. Because such testimonies, and the experiences on which they are based, are powerful and immediate, many people take them to be self-validating. But feelings of well-being, important as they are, are not by themselves accurate, objective measures of health. Mansell Pattison found that most of those who claimed miraculous healing returned to medical doctors within a week or two of the experience. The same was true of a number of healings reported at Fuller. The October, 1982 issue of *Christian Life* had several testimonies of those claiming healing in the Wimber course. Within two weeks of the testimonies being given and before they appeared in print, my wife and I visited one person who had to be taken to the hospital and talked to another who no longer felt well.

Feelings of well-being are influenced by a great many factors. People naturally feel better when others gather around them and make them the focus of their attention. Moreover, God has created in the body processes that work toward health. Christian honesty requires that claims of miraculous healing be delayed until careful examinations are made over longer periods of time, and others must be permitted to investigate those claims. The lack of such testing for objective reality is one of my strong concerns for the current emphasis on healing in the church.

In contrast to many of the healings claimed today, those performed by Christ were instant, dramatic and durable. Those crippled for life walked. Those blind from birth saw and recognized what they saw. Lazarus, who was dead for three days, was brought back to life.

Christian honesty also requires that we report our failures as well and as loudly as we proclaim our successes. Smedes notes,

> To the extent that we are eager to sustain people's interests, hopes and expectations, we are tempted to exaggerate successes and disguise failures . . . . Honesty in a crooked world is not as spectacular as healing in a hurting world, but in the long run it is a stronger sign of God's power.
>
> One requirement of honesty in a public ministry of healing is full and accurate reporting, both to the faithful and to the world-at-large. The minister who engages in healing should publicize his or her failures as loudly as the successes.[37]

Finally, we need to test the source of those healings that do occur. Scripture warns us that not all miracles come from God (Acts 8:9-24; II Thess. 2:3-12), and the voice we hear within us may be our own desires (James 4:1-2; II Pet. 2:15).

Influenced by the spirit of the times, many today take success as a test of what is good and of God. For example, some reported that the class on healing at Fuller was the largest and most popular on campus. The implicit assumption was that this success was evidence of its validity. Few noted that many in the class were not regular students at Fuller, but members of Wimber's church interested only in this one course. Similarly, the rapid growth of the Vineyard church is used to confirm the truth of the message of healing being preached.[38]

Success, however, is a measure of human phenomena, not of theological realities. Many movements are successful, even though they do not proclaim the truth. We must test all ideas and movements in the light of scripture. Unfortunately, such tests are often seen as evidence of unbelief, rather than obedience to the biblical mandate to "test the spirits."

A New Christian Magic

Another danger is to turn healing, miracles, success and prosperity into a new Christian magic. This is one of the fundamental tendencies we have as sinful humans, for magic makes us gods. We feel we are supreme, for we can carry out our will by controlling nature, supernatural powers or even God himself.

Magic is the opposite of religion. In magic, we are in control; in religion, we are in submission to God and his will. The difference between the two is not in practice—it is in attitude. We can pray seeking God's help, or we can pray thinking, often without even admitting it to ourselves, that we can make God do our bidding. We can read the scripture to learn and grow, or we can carry it in our pocket, confident that it will protect us from harm, like an amulet. We pray when our child is seriously ill and ask that God's will be done, but soon find ourselves trying to coerce God to do our bidding. We may not even be fully aware when we shift from one to the other.

One sign of magic is a formula approach. We believe our prayers will be answered if we say the right things and act in certain ways. Scripture instructs us to pray "in the name of Christ," but if we think that our prayers have power only when we utter these words, worship has become magic. To pray in Christ's name is to pray for what he wills in the situation (James 4:3).

Similarly, some argue, despite the example of Jesus, that to add "nevertheless, not my will but thine be done" at the end of a prayer shows lack of faith and weakens the prayer. The fundamental attitude of worship is subordination. In worship, it is important that God's will be done, not that our desires be answered. Faith is not some kind of "power" that controls God. It is entrusting ourselves completely to God's care. In magic, on the other hand, our will is supreme.

Unfortunately, Christian magic is very much a part of our times. One recent tabloid advertisement promises health, money, a job, happiness, success and good fortune to those who pray using the golden cross that will be sent to all enquirers. Other advertisements in the same paper promise health and prosperity to those who write in for the "miraculous Lourdes cross," the "cross of Antron," water from the river Jordan or the special prayers of Rev. Dr. John. One preacher promises those who use the paper "prayer rug" he encloses (on which are written special Bible verses) that they will receive "salvation, joy, love, peace, extra money! new and better homes! new car! putting home back together!—and the desires of their heart!" (exclamation marks in the original). To reassure the readers, the letter has the testimony of a man who started with nothing but now has two restaurants, two motels, a Dairy Cream store, a service station, thirty employees, four cars and three trucks because he used the prayer rug. With the prayer rug comes a book that describes which Bible verses should be "claimed" to gain particular ends.

These are blatant cases of Christian magic and easy to detect. Of greater danger are the subtler forms of magic that creep into our thinking unawares. For example, one media preacher asks people to "sow money seeds in God's fields" by giving to his ministry. He promises that God will repay them a thousand-fold. In so doing, he reduces biblical principles to mechanical formulas. Another leader advocates the saying of certain phrases in prayers of healing to assure positive results. The appeal of magic is great, for it makes us gods.

Reinforcing Secularism

Contradictory as it may seem, by overemphasizing miracles, in the long run we reinforce secularism. To the extent that we focus our attention on the "miraculous" nature of some events and differentiate them from other events viewed as "natural," we reinforce our old Western dualism that consigns God to otherworldly matters and explains natural phenomena purely in scientific terms. If we take this approach, claims of miracles do initially remind us of God's work in this world. As these miracles become routine, however, they lose their impact. They are no longer seen as extraordinary—as *real* miracles. Consequently, we must look for new and ever more spectacular miracles to reassure us that God is with us. In the long run, the net effect of this escalation is the secularization of our thought. We do not see God at work in ordinary, natural processes. As miracles become commonplace, they no longer remind us of God. In the end, the quest for ever new demonstrations of God's presence breaks down, and we are left in a totally secularized world in which there are few ways for God to speak to us.

The answer lies not in seeking miracles, nor in denying them. It is to reject this dichotomy altogether. The answer is to see the *naturalness* of God's extraordinary healings and the *miraculous* nature of his ordinary ones. It is to avoid treating the former as greater signs of God's presence, whether explicitly or implicitly, by making them the center of our church's attention and ministry.

Imbalance

Christian maturity calls for a balanced concern for provision, health, peace, justice and righteousness—a balance that can be maintained only as Christ, not these causes, is at the center. When we rediscover a forgotten truth, we frequently over-accentuate it. The problem is not new. As James Aiken points out, "The church in Corinth overemphasized the miraculous, specifically the gift of tongues. Paul wrote not to frown on gifts, but to pursue balance in exercising them."[39] The same caution against overemphasis needs to be made regarding the current focus on healing.

One danger we must avoid is focusing our attention more on our immediate human needs than on ultimate realities. The result is a new and more subtle form of the social gospel. With a renewed emphasis on God's special work in our everyday lives, we must be on guard lest we lose sight of the greater importance of dealing with sin and divine judgment.

This focus on the "now" is accentuated by our modern Western emphasis on personal needs and fulfillment, and on theories of psychology that order these needs along a scale from physical to psychological, then social and finally spiritual. According to these theories, we can deal with higher level problems only when we have solved those below them. In the church, this can lead us to spend so much time on present human needs that we have little time to deal with sin and righteousness or to focus our attention on God. The amount of time we spend on something reflects its importance in our thinking, no matter what we say to the contrary.

The call of the scriptures is clear: We are called to be disciples of Jesus Christ. Discipleship, not present well-being, is our central message. Christ healed many, but few became his disciples.

A second danger is to emphasize healing, particularly physical healing, and to forget provision, justice, peace and equality. All of them belong to the kingdom of God (Luke 4:18-19). Feeding the hungry and healing the sick were among Jesus' first acts. In a sense, they were easy to carry out and raised little opposition. Far more costly was his condemnation of oppression, injustice and violence, for this, in the end, led to his death.

We too need to emphasize the whole gospel, including those parts that demand suffering and sacrifice on our part. Our temptation is to emphasize the parts that benefit us personally, or to focus our attention on only one aspect, whether this be healing, peace or justice. When we do so, however, we are in danger of shifting the center from Christ to ourselves or to a cause. Christ then is on the margin, and we use him mainly to justify the gospel we preach.

Increasing the Burden

We rejoice when God heals in answer to prayer, and we should do so publicly, but what about those whom God, in his will and foreknowledge, chooses not to heal? What do we say to them, for they are in the greatest need of ministry? If we teach healing but have no answer for those who remain sick or face death, we generate in them a false sense of guilt and despair.

Here Wimber faces a dilemma. He admits that people are often not healed after special prayer. He is not willing, however, to see this as the will of God or to admit that sickness can lead us closer to him. Benn and Burkill write,

> At a ministers' seminar led by one of Wimber's team, one of us asked the question, "Is it ever in the loving will of God to allow His children to suffer for a greater good?" *We received no reply.* Wimber's conclusion towards the end of an otherwise helpful chapter is staggering—"There are many reasons why people are not healed when prayed for. Most of the reasons involve some form of sin and unbelief (*Power Healing*, p. 164). Yet he can *still* say, "I never blame the sick person for lack of faith if healing does not occur" (*Power Healing*, p. 186).[40]

To attribute sickness and death to lack of faith or to Christian defeat (as some claim in the case of David Watson) is too simple an answer (cf. Job; John 9:2; II Cor. 12:7-9). Even more than a theology of healing, we need a theology of suffering and death—one that does not see these as failures but as part of God's greater redemptive work. We also need the grace of godly dying, in which our passing is marked by a God-given serenity, anticipation and hope.

Exalting the Leader

We have already noted that in highly individualistic, culturally pluralistic societies, such as we have in North America, there is a strong tendency to focus on personalities and to exalt leaders. There are few strong social groups that hold people together and no dominant set of shared ideas and values that unite people in their thinking. People are left to fend for themselves, and often they are attracted to a "big man" who claims to know the way.[41] This is true in our modern world of business, politics, entertainment and even the church.

This model of leadership creates a number of problems within the church. It encourages most Christians to be followers prone to trust uncritically what their leaders say. It gives rise to leaders who are not themselves in submission and accountable to others in the church.

Throughout church history, this exaltation of leaders has been most common in movements centered around healing, exorcism and everyday human concerns.[42] Few are tempted to say that the preacher saves the sinner. Many, however, attribute healings to the faith of a particular leader. When others fail, it is to him or her that they take the sick for special prayer.

Healing in the church belongs to the congregation. Some may have the particular gift of praying for the sick, but they do so as members of the body rather than as leaders. Moreover, this is a secondary gift that must be subordinate to worship and the ministry of the Word (I Cor. 12:27-31).

V. HEALING MINISTRIES IN THE CHURCH

What significance does all this have for healing ministries in the church? Certainly scripture commands us to pray for the sick and to take those prayers seriously (James 5:14-15). This should be part of ordinary church life along with prayer for the destitute, the jobless, the homeless, the oppressed and, above all, the lost. Moreover, prayer for the sick should be a part of the evangelistic outreach of the church. What we need is discernment on how to be faithful to scripture and to guard against the fads of our time. Several principles regarding such ministries are found in scripture.

A Pastoral Ministry

At the heart of the ministry of the church is a pastoral heart—a love of people and a willingness to share in their struggles and to help bear their burdens. A church must be concerned with the everyday needs of human life and should minister to these needs in both personal and corporate ways.

There needs to be a ministry to the sick. This is particularly true in urban settings, where people have lost the normal support groups of relatives, neighbors and friends. Mansell Pattison found that for many who sought prayer for healing, the important thing was not that they were physically healed (many were not), but that they felt the support of others in their times of difficulty. As humans, we need the spiritual healing that comes from being loved even more than we need physical well-being.

There needs equally to be a ministry to the oppressed—the poor, the battered, the jobless. They are all around us. They are in our churches, often unseen. And there needs to be a ministry to those society tends to consider marginal—the lonely, the single, the aged, the retarded and handicapped, the migrants. One key measure of the godliness of a society or a church is the way it treats the oppressed and the marginalized. It is for its own advantage that the world takes care of the successful, the powerful and the wealthy. The church, however, is entrusted with the care of the poor, the widows, the orphans, the sick, the oppressed, the wayward, the spiritually immature and the lost. It exists for others. It is not a gathering of the spiritually strong, but a community of broken sinners who have experienced the grace of God and who now minister to others who are broken and lost.

These ministries can take many forms. Special times of prayer can be set aside in certain services for those in need—the sick, the jobless, the sinner seeking forgiveness, the lonely and sad. In the

City Terrace Mennonite Brethren Church, these are invited to come to the front for special prayer once or twice a month. In other churches, this ministry is given to Sunday school classes or to evening services.

Care must be taken, however, not to promise that all will be healed. The expectations of the average Christian are frequently too low with regard to what God will do, but to raise them too high can be destructive to those God chooses not to heal at that moment. Moreover, particular care must be given to those who continue to suffer, for they are in the greatest need of ministry: those whom God chooses not to heal, those who face death, those caught in difficult marriages and the like. For them, the church needs a ministry of hope, assurance and hospitality.[43] It is hard, however, to develop a true ministry of hospitality in our modern churches, for this demands our time—the most precious commodity we have—as well as our resources.

A Teaching Ministry

A second vital ministry in the church, particularly as it has to do with ministries such as healing, is teaching. The older, more mature Christians should be examples and teachers at heart. They must begin where young believers are in their faith, but they must not be content with this. They should instruct, encourage, rebuke and model a godly life, and do so with a firm but gentle spirit. They should seek to settle disputes and strive for unity and harmony in the congregation, balancing the needs of the members as individuals and the needs of the congregation as a whole. They are to avoid empty disputes over words and senseless controversies that breed quarrels (II Tim. 2:14,23), teach with kindness and forbearance, correct opponents with gentleness (II Tim. 2:24-25), and endure criticisms and slander patiently (II Tim. 2:3-7).

Paul himself was an example of this. When a movement of ecstasy swept through the church in Corinth, causing some members to exalt speaking in tongues, healing and other visible manifestations of God's work, Paul took a strong stand, seeking to maintain order and unity in the church.[44] He did not reject the spiritually young for their excesses and their pursuit of the spectacular. Rather, he instructed them in love and firmness to work as one body and to guard lest their behavior bring offense to the gospel in the world around them. And he showed them the higher way of Christian maturity—of love and mutual submission.

Applying these principles to the current emphasis on healing, we should pray freely for the illnesses and other needs of seekers and new believers, knowing that God often works in special ways in the lives of those at the point of deciding for or against Christ. Then, however, we must lead them from the elementary to the deeper things of faith—discipleship, holiness, witnessing and suffering for the sake of the gospel. We must help young believers move from a focus on themselves and their immediate needs to a concern for the lost and suffering world.

We should also seek a balance in our church services. There are times when prayer for healing is appropriate. At the same time, there should be prayers ministering to those who remain sick. In both, we must pray in faith and submit ourselves to the sovereignty of God. The central expectation, however, must be of meeting an omnipotent God. In this, confession of sin, worship and response to God's call to ministry and mission are important parts.

A Prophetic Ministry

Finally, the church has a prophetic calling. It must discern the setting in which God has placed it and speak out against evil. It must also guard lest the church itself become a servant to the spirit of the culture and time in which it lives.

The criteria for making these judgments are not the values of the world, nor even the majority vote of all those who call themselves Christian. The standard must be the Word of God understood and applied by communities of committed believers. Particular responsibility is placed on the leaders (I Tim. 3:9; 6:20; II Tim. 1:12-14; Titus 1:9), who lead their congregations in discerning what God is saying to them and guard the church lest it be deceived (II Thess. 2:9; I Tim. 4:1-7; II Tim. 2:19; 3:1-4:5).

With regard to the current emphasis on healing, the church must test the teachings against scripture and the spirit at work in the services. An uncritical acceptance of either allows the church to be led astray. The church must also challenge the values of our day: the obsession with the self, with the present and with health, success and personal fulfillment. It must guard against popular and pragmatic methods that provide immediate solutions but in the end subvert the gospel. Satan did not challenge God's goal for humans. He simply offered them an instant, easy means to get there.

We who live in the end times face great opportunities and great dangers. In the last days the gospel will be preached to the ends of the earth. There will also be a great falling away as many, including Christians, are deceived. It is important, therefore, that we listen to God as he speaks to us through his Spirit and that we test the voices we hear to make certain that they are, indeed, from God. God has given us his Word to keep and proclaim. May we be found faithful to that trust.

Part
Four

CONCLUSION

In a sense, it is presumptuous to write a conclusion to a book such as this. The conclusion will be lived out in the lives of people, Christians and non-Christians, supporters and detractors of John Wimber. And ultimately, of course, the conclusion will be written by God, who will try each man's work by fire. What is precious will remain; the chaff will be burnt away; and the Christian worker, whatever the merits of his work, will be saved.

In the meantime, we must struggle on in a fallen world, striving to be true to our Lord Jesus Christ and seeking to discern his will. John Wimber is not an evil man. He is a Christian, a believer, a saint and therefore our brother. We affirm him as such. He has done and is continuing to do much good. Many of the strengths and benefits of his work have been highlighted in this book. On the other hand, there are some aspects of John Wimber's understanding that we believe can lead to difficulties and unnecessary suffering in the church. We have tried to point these out also in this book. Our prayer is that this volume will be helpful in separating the precious from the chaff, that it will assist the body of Christ in discerning and obeying the will of God.

James R. Coggins
Paul G. Hiebert

Notes

FOREWORD

1. Cited in Wallace Benn and Mark Burkill, "A theological and pastoral critique of the teachings of John Wimber," *Churchman*, CI, no. 2, (1987), no. 2, pp. 101-102.

THE MAN, THE MOVEMENT AND THE MESSAGE

1. George Marsden, *Reforming Fundamentalism: Fuller Seminary and the New Evangelicalism* (Grand Rapids, MI: Eerdmans, 1987).

2. Paul G. Hiebert, "The flaw of the excluded middle," *Missiology: An International Review*, X, no. 1 (January 1982), pp. 35-47.

3. Tim Stafford, "Testing the Wine from John Wimber's Vineyard," *Christianity Today*, August 8, 1986, p. 18.

4. *Ibid.*

5. Carol Wimber, "A Hunger for God: A Reflective Look at the Vineyard's Beginnings," *The Vineyard Newsletter*, II, no. 3 (Fall, 1987), p. 1.

6. C. Peter Wagner, *The Third Wave of the Holy Spirit: Encountering the Power of Signs and Wonders Today* (Ann Arbor, MI: Servant Publications, 1988).

7. There are 907,000,000 Roman Catholics, 322,000,000 Protestants, 173,000,000 Orthodox and 51,600,00 Anglicans. These figures include nominal Christians. They were cited by David Barrett, editor of the *World Christian Encyclopedia* in conjunction with the North American Congress on the Holy Spirit and World Evangelism. This gathering attracted 40,000 people to New Orleans, July 22-26, 1987 and featured optimistic plans to evangelize the world by the year 2000.

8. Stafford, "Testing the Wine," p. 19.
9. Carol Wimber, "Hunger for God," pp. 1-2.
10. Stafford, "Testing the Wine," p. 19.
11. *Bob Dylan: the man, the music, the message* (Old Tappan, NJ: Fleming H. Revell, 1985).
12. Carol Wimber, "Hunger for God," pp. 3,7.
13. John White, "MC510: A Look Inside," *First Fruits,* July-August 1985, September-October 1985.
14. C. Peter Wagner, ed., *Signs and Wonders Today* (Altamonte Springs, FL: Creation House, 1987), pp. 6, 152.
15. Lewis B. Smedes, ed., *Ministry and the Miraculous: A Case Study at Fuller Theological Seminary* (Pasadena, CA.: Fuller Theological Seminary, 1987).
16. Ken Blue, *Authority to Heal* (Downers Grove, Ill.: InterVarsity Press, 1987); John White, *When the Spirit Comes with Power: Signs & Wonders among God's People* (Downers Grove, Ill.: InterVarsity Press, 1988).
17. London: Hodder and Stoughton, 1985; reprinted by Harper and Row, 1986.
18. San Francisco: Harper and Row, 1986.
19. Wimber associates giving seminars have included Blaine Cook, Ed Piorek, Carl Tuttle, Chuck Apperson, Lance Pittluck, Rick Martinez, Lee Bennett, Mike Cramer, Rick Olmstead, Randy Clark, Bob Craine, John McClure and Mike Turrigiano. As of 1988, however, VMI has ceased to sponsor seminars by these others, concentrating on seminars led by Wimber himself.
20. In early 1988, Sam Thompson was the U.S. pastoral coordinator and regional coordinators were Lee Bennett, Bob Craine, Kenn Gulliksen, Todd Hunter, John McClure, Brent Rue and Tom Stipe. See *The Vineyard Newsletter,* III, no. 1 (Winter, 1988), pp. 2,5,7.
21. Sam Thompson, "A Vineyard Overview," *The Vineyard Newsletter,* III, no. 1 (Winter, 1988), pp. 5,7. Cf. "Theological and Philosophical Statements," *Vineyard Training Manual* (1986), in which the 10,000 figure is to be achieved "in our generation."

WIMBER, WORD AND SPIRIT

1. Quoted in Tim Stafford, "Testing the Wine from John Wimber's Vineyard," *Christianity Today* (August 8, 1986), p. 21.
2. John C. Olin, ed., *John Calvin and Jacopo Sadoleto: A Reformation Debate* (New York, 1966), p. 61.
3. Walter Elliott, ed. and trans., *The Sermons and Conferences of John Tauler* (Washington, DC, 1910), p. 658.
4. *Ibid.,* p. 505.
5. See Ernst Cassirer, Paul Oskar Kristeller and John Herman Randall, eds., *The Renaissance Philosophy of Man* (Chicago: 1948), p. 111.
6. Peter Brown, *Augustine of Hippo* (Berkeley and Los Angeles: 1967), p. 168.
7. From Pico della Mirandola's, "Oration on the Dignity of Man."
8. Walter Elliott,*Tauler,* p. 132.
9. *Ibid.,* p. 135.
10. *Ibid.,* p. 82.
11. *Ibid.,* p. 353.

12. *Ibid.*, p. 72.
13. *Ibid.*, p. 31.
14. *Ibid.*, p. 353.
15. Guenther Franz, ed., *Thomas Muentzer. Schriften und Briefe* (Guetersloh, 1968), p. 398.
16. See Lewis' article in this volume.
17. See my essay on "Thomas Muentzer and Martin Luther," *Archiv fuer Reformationsgeschichte* (1987).
18. David Hunt and T.A. McMahon, *The Seduction of Christianity: Spiritual Discernment in the Last Days* (Eugene, OR: Harvest House, 1985), p. 179.

THE POWER OF PIETISM

1. *Pia Desideria* (Philadelphia, PA: Fortress Press), p. 117.
2. For more information on Pietism see Peter C. Erb, ed., *Pietists: Selected Writings* (New York: Paulist Press, 1983); and Dale Brown, *Understanding Pietism* (Grand Rapids, MI: Wm.B. Eerdmans, 1978). Information on relations between Pietism and the Mennonite tradition is available in Robert Friedmann, *Mennonite Piety through the Centuries, Its Genius and its Literature* (Mennonite Historical Society, 1949). See also David Ewert's fine article, "Reading the Bible through coloured glass," *Mennonite Brethren Herald* (October 30, 1987), pp. 6-9.

THE ROLE OF EMOTIONS IN CHRISTIAN FAITH

1. G.C. Oosthuizen, *Post Christianity in Africa* (Grand Rapids, MI: Wm.B. Eerdmans, 1968), pp. 151, 159n.
2. Fredrick Morgan Davenport, *Primitive Traits in Religious Revivals* (New York: MacMillan Co., 1917), p. 142.
3. Hoell N. Bloch, *The Pentecostal Movement* (Oslo: Universite forlaget, 1964), p. 9n.
4. Robert H. Thouless, *The Psychology of Religion* (Cambridge: Cambridge University Press, 1923), p. 155.
5. Davenport, pp. 114-115, 130-131.
6. Nehemiah Curnock, *The Journal of John Wesley* (London: The Epworth Press, 1938), VII, p. 153.
7. William G. McLoughlin Jr., *Modern Revivalism* (New York: Ronald Press, 1959), pp. 132, 147.
8. Morton T. Kelsey, *Discernment: A Study in Ecstasy and Evil* (New York: Paulist Press, 1978), pp. 20-25.
9. McLoughlin, pp. 132, 147.
10. Bernard A. Weisberger, *They Gathered at the River* (Boston: Little, Brown and Co., 1958), p. 36.
11. William James, *The Varieties of Religious Experience* (New York: Longmans, Green and Co., 1928), pp. 243-56.

AN HISTORIAN'S ASSESSMENT

1. John Wimber and Kevin Springer, *Power Healing* (London: Hodder and Stoughton, 1986), pp. 164-67.

2. John Wimber and Kevin Springer, *Power Evangelism* (San Francisco: Harper and Row, 1986), p. 74.

3. John Wimber, *Signs, Wonders and Church Growth* (Placentia, CA: Vineyard Ministries International, n.d.), section 3, p. 7.

4. J.I. Packer, "Signs and Wonders: Interview," *Touchstone* (a local newspaper in Vancouver, BC, January 1986), p. 7.

5. *Ibid.*

NEW WINE FROM THE VINEYARD

1. Ben Patterson, "Cause for Concern," *Christianity Today* (August 8, 1986), p. 20.

2. John Wimber, *Power Evangelism,* (London: Hodder and Stoughton, 1985), p. 19.

3. "Vineyard Vision."

4. John Wimber, *Power Evangelism,* p. 19.

5. *Ibid.,* p. 20.

6. Wilbert R. Shenk, ed., *Exploring Church Growth* (Grand Rapids, MI: Eerdmans, 1983), pp. 211-12.

7. G.W Peters, *A Theology of Church Growth* (Grand Rapids, MI: Zondervan, 1981), pp. 36-37.

8. Ralph H. Elliott, *Church Growth That Counts* (Valley Forge, PA: Judson Press, 1982), p. 69.

9. Lewis B. Smedes, ed., *Ministry and the Miraculous* (Pasadena, CA: Fuller Theological Seminary, 1987), p. 26.

10. *Ibid.,* pp. 29-30.

11. G.W. Peters *A Theology of Church Growth,* p. 160.

12. J.I. Packer "Signs and Wonders: Interview," *Touchstone* (January 1986), p. 7.

13. *Ibid.*

14. *Mennonite Brethren Herald* (April 4, 1986), p. 5.

15. Lewis B. Smedes, *Ministry and the Miraculous,* p. 51.

16. McNutt, *Healing* (Notre Dame, IN: Ave Maria Press, 1974), p. 74.

17. *The Power to Heal* (Notre Dame, IN: Ave Maria Press, 1977), pp. 134-36.

18. Lewis B. Smedes, *Ministry and the Miraculous,* p. 51.

19. See *First Fruits,* July/August 1987.

20. John Wimber, *Power Evangelism,* p. 46.

21. Larry L. Rose and C. Kirk Hadaway, *The Urban Challenge* (Nashville, TN: Broadman Press, 1982), p. 55.

22. "John Wimber: Signs and Wonders?" *Channels* (Spring 1986), p. 10.

23. Donald McGavian, "The Total Picture," *Christian Life* (October 1982), p. 39.

24. Colin Braun, *That You May Believe* (Grand Rapids, MI: Eerdmans, 1985), p. 60.

25. *Ibid.,* p. 216.

26. John Wimber, *Power Evangelism,* p. 56.

27. *Ibid.*, p. 57.
28. C.S. Lovett, *Jesus Wants You Well* (Baldwin Park, CA: Personal Christianity, 1973), p. 26.
29. Colin Brown, *That You May Believe*, p. 208.
30. John Wimber, *Power Evangelism*, p. 94.
31. Walter Unger, "Signs and Wonders—Wesley, White and Wimber," *Mennonite Brethren Herald (June 12, 1987), pp. 26-27.*
32. McNutt, *The Power to Heal*, pp. 37ff.
33. Al Camponi, "Toward a Balanced View of Healing," unpublished research paper, Mennonite Brethren Biblical Seminary (January 1984), p. 17.
34. Colin Brown, *That You May Believe*, p. 195.
35. Michael Green, *I Believe in the Holy Spirit* (Grand Rapids, MI: Eerdmans, 1975), p. 176.
36. Colin Brown, *That You May Believe*, p. 209.
37. Class notes, "Church Growth I," Fuller Theological Seminary, p. 5.
38. Quoted by J.I. Packer, "Signs and Wonders: Interview," p. 6.
39. David Hubbard, "Hazarding the Risks," *Christian Life* (October 1982), p. 37.

THE MIRACULOUS IN MINISTRY

1. Francis Aloysius Sullivan, *Charisms and Charismatic Renewal: A Biblical and Theological Study* (Ann Arbor, MI: Servant Books, 1982), p. 25.
2. Thomas F. Best, "St. Paul and the Decline of the Miraculous," *East Asia Journal of Theology*, IV, no. 1 (1986), p. 68.
3. *Ibid.*, p. 74.
4. George Slayer Barrett, *The First Epistle General of St. John: A Devotional Commentary* (London: Religious Tract Society, 1910), p. 152.
5. E.M. Blaiklock, *Faith is the Victory: Studies in the First Epistle of John* (Grand Rapids, MI: Eerdmans, 1959), p. 53.

HEALING AND THE KINGDOM

1. Norman Cohn, *The Pursuit of the Millenium* (Oxford: Oxford University Press, 1957).
2. *Ibid.*, pp. 281-6.
3. Max Weber, *The Protestant Ethic and the Spirit of Capitalism*, (trans. Talcott Parsons (New York: Scribner, 1958).
4. Allan Bloom, *The Closing of the American Mind* (New York: Simon and Schuster, 1987), p. 173.
5. Jackson Lears, *The Culture of Consumption*, eds. R.W. Fox and T.J.J. Lears (New York: Pantheon, 1983), p. 4.
6. Walter Tony, *Need the New Religion* (Downers Grove, IL: InterVarsity Press, 1985).
7. Allan Bloom, *The Closing of the American Mind*.
8. Harry Emerson Fosdick, *Twelve Tests of Character* (New York: Association Press, 1923), p. 47.

9. Bruce Barton, *The Man Nobody Knows* (Indianapolis: Bobbs-Merrill, 1925), pp. 143, 149, 151.

10.Gene Ewing, *If You Want Money, A Home in Heaven, Health and Happiness, Based on the Holy Bible, Do These Things* (Atlanta, GA: Rev. Gene Ewing, 1981), p. 5.

11. Huston Smith, *Beyond the Post-Modern Mind* (New York: Crossroad, 1982).

12. Mircea Eliade, *Shamanism: Archaic Techniques of Ecstasy* (Princeton, NJ: Princeton University Press, 1964).

13.Cf. Joanna Michaelsen, *The Beautiful Side of Evil* (Eugene, OR: Harvest House, 1982).

14. C.A. Coulson, *Science and Christian Belief* (London: Collins, 1955).

15. Douglas R. Groothuis, *Unmasking the New Age* (Downers Grove, IL: Intervarsity Press); Karen Hoyt, *The New Age Rage* (Old Tappan, NJ: Fleming H. Revell, 1987).

16. *Ibid.*

17. Douglas R. Groothuis, *Unmasking the New Age* pp. 57-70.

18. David Hunt and T.A. McMahon, *The Seduction of Christianity: Spiritual Discernment in the Last Days* (Eugene, OR: Harvest House, 1985).

19. Wallace Benn and Mark Burkill, "A theological and pastoral critique of the teachings of John Wimber," *Churchman*, CI, no. 2, (1987), pp. 102-3.

20. John Bright, *The Kingdom of God* (Nashville, TN: Abingdon Press, 1953), p. 235.

21. David Ewert, *The Holy Spirit in the New Testament* (Scottdale, PA: Herald Press, 1983), p. 185.

22. J. Denny, "The Theology of the Epistle to the Romans," *The Expositor*, IV, p. 426.

23. John Wimber, *Power Evangelism* (San Francisco: Harper and Row, 1986), p. 107.

24. *Ibid.*

25. Norman Cohn, *The Pursuit of the Millenium.*

26. Robert Bellah et. al., *Habits of the Heart: Individualism and Commitment in American Life* (Berkeley: University of California Press, 1985); Allan Bloom, *The Closing of the American Mind,* pp. 173-84.

27. Bright, *The Kingdom of God,* p. 218.

28. E. Gilchrist, "Baba Farid," *Outreach to Islam* III, 32, (1987).

29. Zella M. Williams, "Testimony of Christian Science Healing," *Christian Science Sentinel*, LXXXVIII, no. 34, 1952.

30. David Martyn Lloyd-Jones, *Prove All Things* (London: Kingsway Publishers, 1986), p. 97.

31. C. Norman Kraus, *The Authentic Witness: Credibility and Authority* (Grand Rapids, MI: Eerdmans, 1979).

32. Benn and Burkill, p. 102.

33. *Ibid.*

34. Cf. David Watson, *Fear No Evil: One Man Deals With Terminal Illness* (Wheaton, IL: Harold Shaw Publishers, 1985).

35. Ernest Becker, *Denial of Death* New York : Free Press, 1973).

36. Jonathan Edwards, *Religious Affections* (New Haven, CT: Yale University Press, 1959), pp. 127-181.

37. Lewis B. Smedes, ed., *Ministry and the Miraculous: A Case Study at Fuller Theological Seminary* (Pasadena, CA: Fuller Theological Seminary, 1987), p. 76.

38. John Wimber, *Power Healing* (San Francisco: Harper and Row, 1986).

39. James Aiken, "Charismatic Mennonites, heresy or hope?" *The Christian Leader*, L, no. 16 (September 29, 1987), p. 6.

40. Benn and Burkill, p. 103, italics in the original.

41. Mary Douglas, *Natural Symbols: Explorations in Cosmology* (New York: Vintage Books, 1970).

42. Norman Cohn, *The Pursuit of the Millenium*.

43. Mortimer Arias, "Centripetal mission or evangelism by hospitality," *Missiology*, X (1982), pp. 69-81.

44. Ralph Martins, *The Spirit and the Congregation: Studies in I Corinthians 12-15* (Grand Rapids, MI: Eerdmans, 1984).